SADISM

Sadism: Psychoanalytic Developmental Perspectives is founded on the premise that paying close attention to what is happening in our internal world can help us understand the rise of sadism in the world of popular culture. Voyeuristic sadism as a form of entertainment appears to be on the rise, an increase corresponding with an upsurge in public appetite for sadomasochism as a recreational activity. This book acts as a forum in which psychotherapists present psychoanalytic perspectives on the phenomenon of sadomasochism at different stages of the human lifecycle: in childhood, adolescence, adulthood and in later life, and consider its developmental roots.

Over the last half-century, through books, movies, computerized video games and drama, the stories we are being sold as representing aspects of contemporary culture market two commodities: sadism and victory. How might we understand this, and can psychoanalysis help us make meaning of this aspect of human relating?

This book does not seek to provide an explanation or a theory of sadomasochism. Instead, *Sadism: Psychoanalytic Developmental Perspectives* offers a thinking space in which we might further our understanding of the developmental origins of sadomasochistic relating and how this can manifest at different life-stages.

Edited by **Amita Sehgal**, with contributions from **Graham Music, Damian McCann, Morit Heitzler, Valerie Sinason, Richard Curen, Brett Kahr, Susan Irving, John Miller and Sandra Evans**.

> A briefing from how clinicians working with a variety of ages and backgrounds are now understanding the tricky territory of sadism; how it lives within us and how to engage with its tentacles. There is something here for practitioners of every background and specialist interest who will learn about the twist of this painful psychic expression.
>
> —**Susie Orbach**, author of *In Therapy*

> This is a unique and important set of essays. Sadism is so often understood in the context of individual pathology but this stimulating volume firmly places sadism into a social, relational and developmental context, thereby deeply enriching our clinical understanding of some of these most disturbing and challenging cases.
>
> —**Susanna Abse**, Couple Psychoanalytic Psychotherapist and CEO Tavistock Relationships (2006–2016)

FORENSIC PSYCHOTHERAPY MONOGRAPH SERIES

Series Editor: Professor Brett Kahr
Honorary Consultant: Dr Estela V. Welldon

Other titles in the Series

SADISM
PSYCHOANALYTIC
DEVELOPMENTAL
PERSPECTIVES

Edited by
Amita Sehgal

Routledge
Taylor & Francis Group

LONDON AND NEW YORK

First published 2018
by Routledge
2 Park Square, Milton Park, Abingdon, Oxon OX14 4RN

and by Routledge
711 Third Avenue, New York, NY 10017

Routledge is an imprint of the Taylor & Francis Group, an informa business

British Library Cataloguing-in-Publication Data
A catalogue record for this book is available from the British Library

Library of Congress Cataloging-in-Publication Data
A catalog record has been requested for this book

ISBN: 978-1-78220-637-8 (pbk)

Typeset in Palatino LT Std
by Medlar Publishing Solutions Pvt Ltd, India

CONTENTS

v

ACKNOWLEDGEMENTS

Putting together a book on a complex subject like sadism (and sado-masochistic relating) is intellectually, emotionally and technically challenging. Editors face the task of assembling a range of perspectives in ways that are coherent, multi-faceted and engaging, while doing justice to the issues raised by different authors. I hope I have successfully accomplished this assignment but ultimately it is for others, the readers of this book, to decide. However, I have not been on my own in addressing the challenge. While the responsibility for the edited outcome is mine alone I do want to acknowledge the help and support I have received from a number of people along the way.

First, it is important to say that the idea for this book germinated from a creative initiative taken by Jane Ryan, Director of Confer, who organised a stimulating series of public talks on sadism. As the founder of Confer, Jane has made an enormous contribution to the mental health community in Great Britain, and I am pleased to have collaborated with her.

Next, I offer my warmest thanks to Professor Brett Kahr, the Series Editor of the "Forensic Psychotherapy Monograph Series", initially at Karnac Books, and now at Routledge, who provided the much appreciated encouragement and support that enabled me to get started on and ultimately complete the project. Brett has been the most facilitative of colleagues and I have greatly valued and benefitted from his advice in steering me through the on-going complexities that have arisen throughout the production of this book.

I extend heartfelt thanks to my close colleague and collaborator, Dr Christopher Clulow, who offered valuable suggestions on structuring the book and on assembling the different contributions. I am grateful to him for helping me successfully navigate the various challenging situations that arose during the process of putting this book together.

I also want to thank Mrs Christel Buss-Twachtmann, Mrs Mary Eckert and Mr Philip Crockatt for generating, and engaging in, stimulating discussions about sadism and sado-masochistic relating, and for deepening my psychoanalytic understanding on this subject.

At the heart of the book, of course, lies the proficiency of talented and well-informed clinicians who, drawing upon the experiences of patients with whom they have worked, have shared their clinical expertise and understanding to shed light on a complex subject. I have very much enjoyed and learned from working with them, and thank them for their help and forbearance in putting this volume together.

I also want to thank the staff at both Karnac Books and at Routledge who have helped in bringing this book to fruition. In particular, I wish to express my appreciation to Oliver Rathbone, the former publisher of Karnac Books, and his team, and more recently, Charles Bath at Routledge who has eased the publication process with good humour and consummate skill.

Finally, and most importantly, I want to thank my husband, John, for his support and continual encouragement throughout the process of working on this book. I am deeply grateful to him for providing a warm and loving environment in which this book on sadism was conceived, worked on and ultimately brought to completion.

SERIES EDITOR'S FOREWORD

While nothing vexes a biomedical researcher more than *carcinoma*, nothing troubles a mental health practitioner more than *sadism*, that destructive urge or impulse which seethes beneath the surface of so much human cruelty and destructiveness. Indeed, I have come to regard sadism as the veritable of cancer of human psychology. Once the sadistic streak becomes activated, it spreads, oozing deadliness in the most indiscriminate and, often, unstoppable manner. And just as physicians struggle to find truly effective treatments for cancer, so, too, do psychotherapeutic workers endeavour to discover the best way to prevent and cure patients propelled by sadistic tendencies.

As early as 1905, in his remarkably frank text *Drei Abhandlungen zur Sexualtheorie* [*Three Essays on the Theory of Sexuality*], Professor Sigmund Freud (1905) described sadism not only as a form of attack upon another person but, also, as a particularly *sexualised* form of attack. Controversially, he came to regard sadism and its variant, sadomasochism, as manifestations of cruelty, which often provide deep excitement within both the mind and the genitalia. Indeed, Freud characterised sadism as the most frequent form of harm inflicted upon the object.

Across the decades, numerous psychoanalytical practitioners have investigated the understanding and treatment of sadism in its many manifestations (e.g., Federn, 1913; Schindler, 1926; Glover, 1964; Ross, 1997; Welldon, 2002, 2016; Miller, 2013; Kahr, 2018). But, just as with carcinoma, no one has yet developed a completely comprehensive means of removing this all too pervasive human propensity from our midst. The forward-thinking American psychohistorian Lloyd deMause (1973, 1974, 1982, 1990, 2002) has, over a long lifetime of scholarship, provided a very convincing theory about the way in which sadism and warfare on the international stage can be traced to early experiences of childhood cruelty. DeMause has argued that sadistic parents produce sadistic adults who become, in turn, sadistic leaders and sadistic followers. He has averred that only through an improvement in the quality of care offered by mothers and fathers will children grow into more emotionally healthy individuals who will become less likely to perpetrate acts of sadism either in intimate spheres or in the political arena.

In spite of the rich feast of psychoanalytical literature on sadism and its origins—brimming with promising avenues for thought and reflection—we still live in a world in which sadism seems to know no bounds, whether in the violence which unfolds in the domestic sphere or in the mayhem which explodes upon the battlefield. Therefore, we still welcome, indeed, *require*, fresh lenses to help us decipher the complex dynamics of this ugly feature of human life.

Happily, Dr Amita Sehgal has produced a truly groundbreaking book in which she and her very experienced contributors have provided us with a map of the psychodynamics of sadism in a multitude of contexts—whether in the mind of the individual or in the nexus of a marriage or a family—across the life cycle. Sehgal has constructed her edited book along developmental lines, providing us with a greater sense of the ways in which sadism emerges throughout infancy and beyond.

Although Sehgal's book will be of great interest to the general student of psychoanalytical psychology, it will be of particular relevance to those who work within the arena of forensic mental health, struggling daily at the coalface with some of our most troubled, disinhibited, and dangerous of patients. Consequently, it pleases me greatly that this book will be included in our "Forensic Psychotherapy Monograph Series", now in its twenty-first year of publication.

I thank Amita Sehgal and the seasoned chapter-writers for sharing their expertise in such a generous way, and I hope that we can all absorb and apply the fruits of their hard-won clinical experiences in our daily practice.

Professor Brett Kahr,
Series Editor,
London.

February, 2018

References

deMause, L. (1973). The history of childhood: the basis for psychohistory. *History of Childhood Quarterly, 1*: 1–3.

deMause, L. (1974). The evolution of childhood. In: L. deMause (Ed.), *The History of Childhood* (pp. 1–73). New York: Psychohistory Press.

deMause, L. (1982). *Foundations of Psychohistory*. New York: Creative Roots.

deMause, L. (1990). The history of child assault. *Journal of Psychohistory, 18*: 1–29.

deMause, L. (2002). *The Emotional Life of Nations*. New York: Karnac/Other Press.

Federn, P. (1913). Beiträge zur Analyse des Sadismus und Masochismus: I. Die Quellen des männlichen Sadismus. *Internationale Zeitschrift für ärztliche Psychoanalyse, 1*: 29–49.

Freud, S. (1905). *Drei Abhandlungen zur Sexualtheorie*. Vienna: Franz Deuticke.

Glover, E. (1964). Aggression and sado-masochism. In: I. Rosen (Ed.), *The Pathology and Treatment of Sexual Deviation: A Methodological Approach* (pp. 146–163). London: Oxford University Press.

Kahr, B. (2018). Committing crimes without breaking the law: unconscious sadism in the "non-forensic" patient. In: B. Kahr (Ed.), *New Horizons in Forensic Psychotherapy: Exploring the Work of Estela V. Welldon* (pp. 239–261). London: Karnac Books.

Miller, J. F. (2013). *The Triumphant Victim: A Psychoanalytical Perspective on Sadomasochism and Perverse Thinking*. London: Karnac Books.

Ross, J. M. (1997). *The Sadomasochism of Everyday Life: Why We Hurt Ourselves – and Others – and How to Stop*. New York: Simon and Schuster.

Schindler, W. (1926). Zur Dynamik des Sadomasochismus. *Fortschritte der Sexualwissenschaft und Psychanalyse, 2*: 127–195.

Welldon, E. V. (2002). *Sadomasochism*. Duxford, Cambridge: Icon Books.

Welldon, E. V. (2016). *Sadomasochism in Art and Politics*. n.p.: n.p.

Richard Curen is a psychotherapist, consultant, and trainer. He has worked at Respond since 2002, first as its chief executive and then as its consultant forensic psychotherapist. Respond is a London-based voluntary-sector organisation providing psychotherapeutically informed services for children and adults with learning disabilities or autism who have experienced abuse or trauma and those who have abused others. Richard oversees all of Respond's forensic services and also consults to a number of organisations and statutory teams working with adolescents and adults with sexually harmful and/or offending behaviours. He has worked in the sexual violence field since 1995 as a psychotherapist, trainer, and manager. Richard is registered with the British Psychoanalytical Council and the British Association for Counselling and Psychotherapy. He is a board member of the International Association for Forensic Psychotherapy, a member of the Forensic Psychotherapy Society, and a member of the Institute of Psychotherapy and Disability.

Sandra Evans trained in general and old age psychiatry and, although now retired from her NHS post, she is still clinically active. She is a group analyst and continues to work with groups in private practice. She is an academic with interests in teaching, pastoral care and mentoring, and in psychoanalysis. She co-edited the book *Talking Over the Years* (2004) with Jane Garner, and is working on a new edited volume with colleagues addressing psychoanalytic understanding of dementia and caring. She is chair of the older adults section of the Association of Psychoanalytic Psychotherapy in the NHS.

Morit Heitzler is a psychotherapist, supervisor, and trainer with a private practice in Oxford. She offers both short- and long-term work with a wide range of clients from diverse backgrounds. Morit specialises in trauma work, and has developed her own integrative approach, incorporating—within an overall relational perspective—somatic trauma therapy, body psychotherapy, attachment theory, sensorimotor work, eye movement desensitisation and reprocessing (EMDR), modern neuroscience, and family constellations. In a wide range of contexts, both in the UK and in Israel, including the Traumatic Stress Service of the Maudsley Hospital in London and at the Oxford Stress and Trauma Centre, Morit has gained a wealth of experience in working with traumatised clients, including refugees and asylum-seekers, suffering from a wide variety of post-traumatic symptoms. Her contributions to the profession include teaching on various training courses in the UK and in Israel, and regularly leading workshops and groups.

Susan Irving worked in acute psychiatry as a social worker before training as a psychoanalytic psychotherapist in the 1980s with the British Association of Psychotherapists. She worked in private practice and the NHS until 2003, and then trained as a couple psychoanalytic psychotherapist at Tavistock Relationships, where she has subsequently been employed to lead both theoretical and clinical seminars.

She has additionally been accepted as a full member of the British Psychoanalytic Association and works in London and Cornwall in private practice as a couple therapist and psychoanalyst.

Brett Kahr is senior fellow at Tavistock Relationships at the Tavistock Institute of Medical Psychology in London and also senior clinical research fellow in psychotherapy and mental health at the Centre for Child Mental Health in London. He is a consultant psychotherapist at the Balint Consultancy in London, and visiting professor in the Faculty of Media and Communication at Bournemouth University, as well as consultant in psychology to the Bowlby Centre. He held two terms of office as chair of the Society of Couple Psychoanalytic Psychotherapists, and then held three further terms as founding chair of the British Society of Couple Psychotherapists and Counsellors, the professional association of the Tavistock Centre for Couple Relationships. A member of the editorial board of *Couple and Family Psychoanalysis*, he is a series co-editor of the Library of Couple and Family Psychoanalysis for Karnac Books, as well as founding series editor of the Forensic Psycho-therapy monograph series. Author or editor of nine books, including *Sex and the Psyche*, he has published, most recently, *Life Lessons from Freud*, and also *Tea with Winnicott* and *Coffee with Freud*. A trustee to the Freud Museum, he works with individuals and couples in Hampstead, north London.

Damian McCann is a qualified systemic practitioner, supervisor, and trainer, and a qualified couple psychoanalytic psychotherapist. He is currently employed as a consultant systemic psychotherapist at a child and adolescent mental health service within the NHS and is head of service development and learning at Tavistock Relationships. He is an associate of Pink Therapy, where he was co-director of the post-graduate diploma in relationship therapy with gender and sexual diversities. He has a particular interest in working with violence and abuse within couple relationships, and his clinical doctorate was concerned with understanding the meaning and impact of violence and abuse within same-sex relationships. He is in private practice working as a couple psychotherapist and supervisor.

John Miller is a psychoanalyst and psychotherapist with a special inter-est and experience in education and children's learning and behavioural problems. He read psychology and philosophy at St Catherine's College, Oxford, and did his post-graduate training in educational psychology at the Tavistock Clinic. Previously a consultant to numerous schools and organisations for deprived and troubled children in different parts of Britain, as well as Norway, Belgium, and France, he has been a mem-ber of the International Association for Analytical Psychology for over thirty years, and training analyst to various psychotherapy trainings. He has a full-time practice in Oxford. His book *The Triumphant Victim*, a study of sadomasochism, was published in 2013, and *Do You Read Me?*, about understanding children's learning problems, in 2015.

Graham Music is consultant child and adolescent psychotherapist at the Tavistock and Portman Clinics and an adult psychotherapist in private practice. His publications include *Nurturing Natures: Attachment and Children's Emotional, Sociocultural and Brain Development* (2010), *Affect and Emotion* (2001), and *The Good Life: Wellbeing and the New Science of Altruism, Selfishness and Immorality* (2014). He has a particular interest in exploring the interface between developmental findings and clinical work. Formerly associate clinical director of the Tavistock's Child and Family Department, he has managed a range of services working with the aftermath of child maltreatment and neglect, and he has organised many community-based psychotherapy services. He currently works clinically with forensic cases at the Portman Clinic. He teaches, lectures, and supervises on a range of trainings in Britain and abroad.

Amita Sehgal is a couple psychoanalytic psychotherapist accredited by the British Psychoanalytic Council. She is a visiting lecturer at Tavistock Relationships, London, and a consultant psychotherapist at the Balint Consultancy, London. Amita has a special interest in the neurobiology of contemporary attachment perspectives in couple psychotherapy. Amita's ongoing interest in the psychological process of separation and divorce informs her commitment to resolving family disputes out of court, in a non-confrontational and constructive manner. She also consults to family lawyers on strengthening client–lawyer relationships, as well as on the emotional impact of family work on themselves as legal professionals. Amita has published in the field of couple psychotherapy. She maintains a private practice in central London.

Valerie Sinason is a poet, writer, child and adult psychotherapist, and adult psychoanalyst. She is the founder of the Clinic for Dissociative Studies, president of the Institute of Psychotherapy and Disability, and honorary consultant psychotherapist at Cape Town Child Guidance Clinic. She was a consultant psychotherapist at the Tavistock Clinic and the Portman Clinic, the Anna Freud Centre, and St George's Hospital. In 2016, she was awarded the lifetime achievement award by the International Society for the Study of Trauma and Dissociation. Widely published, her most recent book is *Shattered but Unbroken: Voices of Triumph and Testimony* (2016).

INTRODUCTION

Amita Sehgal

Voyeuristic sadism as a form of entertainment seems to be on the rise, the increase corresponding with an upsurge in public appetite for sadomasochism as a recreational activity. Such stories in popular culture, whether these are written or performed in cinematic or theatrical form, tend to be morality plays pitching good against evil. In these stories, evil tends towards extreme and accentuated forms of sadism, and the destruction of evil (and its sadistic extremes) becomes the victorious denouement (Carroll, 2011).

The skilful commercialisation of story-telling, which began in the late nineteenth century, has over the last fifty years or so led to its industrialisation: technological advances in television and film-making have resulted in a predictable formula of good and evil being packaged in episodic units of time and delivered to television and film audiences worldwide. During this allocated time, story-tellers and script-writers influence their audiences by delaying the relief that can accompany victory when good triumphs over evil, perhaps constituting a sadistic enactment in itself.

Interestingly, over the last half-century, trends within the entertainment industry also seem to have swung more towards sadism (and horror). A good example of this is the popular James Bond films that depict the adventures of the fictional character of the same name created by novelist Ian Fleming in 1953. Bond is a British secret agent working for his country's foreign intelligence agency, the Military Intelligence Section 6, commonly known as MI6. He has been portrayed on film in twenty-six productions made between 1962 and 2015. As a mortal superhero, Bond has shifted from being depicted as having *savoir-faire* and wit (between 1962 and 1983) to having a much darker character, more ruthless and humourless (from 2005 to 2015). These later films have sadistic acts liberally sprinkled throughout the storyline, and victory is reduced to mere survival. Interestingly, though, in comic-book portrayals of superheroes perpetuating the theme of good being victorious over evil, the use of two-dimensional cartoon characters and incredulous situations removes the sting from sadism because the reader does not identify with the pain being inflicted.

Over the last twenty-five years, American film-maker Quentin Tarantino's films have achieved great critical and commercial success. In his films, spanning 1992 to 2015, Tarantino has moved away from depictions of crime-related violence to sadism and gore more firmly rooted in the horror genre. In his first three films, *Reservoir Dogs* (1992), *Pulp Fiction* (1994), and *Jackie Brown* (1997), viewers are treated to fascinating, witty dialogue by protagonists who speak casually about what is on their minds just before they commit heinous crimes. These characters are heard to engage in banal conversation in the preamble to the attacks either because they have arrived too early at the scene, or are in the process of getting ready to carry out the planned violence. For example, the opening diner scene in *Reservoir Dogs* (1992) shows six ruthless gangsters analysing a popular frothy pop song, "Like a Virgin" (1984) by American singer Madonna, with tremendous seriousness prior to carrying out a horrifically violent and bloody bank robbery. Similarly, in *Pulp Fiction*, two of the protagonists arrive somewhat early to the scene where they will proceed to scare, torture, and kill. But, as they wait to begin, they pass the time by discussing their foot-massage techniques.

Tarantino's early films seem to present gun violence in a way that can seem surreal and distancing to the viewer. However, in his more recent films like *Django Unchained* (2012) and *The Hateful Eight* (2015), Tarantino's depiction of violence is more realistic. The descent into intense, visceral, gruesome violence is not prefaced by dialogue but by visual gore. Having said that, throughout all of Tarantino's films, his portrayal of violence as a source of unabashed pleasure is unsettling.

Reservoir Dogs (1992), for instance, is best remembered for the scene depicting the sadistic torture of a captured policeman tied to a chair and doused in petrol: here, the menacing tormentor appears to relish in the pain and anguish of his victim as he slices off his captive's ear whilst dancing to the tune of a pop song playing on the radio.

On the television screen, too, sadism appears as a vital ingredient in Scandinavian noir, the genre comprising the adaptation of crime fiction and screenplays written by Nordic writers for films and television series. A notable example is the Danish television psychological thriller series *The Killing* (2007) that was first broadcast on Danish national television in January 2007. Since then, it has been transmitted in many countries worldwide, garnering significant critical acclaim. Each series is set in Copenhagen and tracks, in dark tones, a murder case day by day.

Another good example is *Game of Thrones*, a critically acclaimed American drama series that is an adaptation of a set of fantasy novels written by George Martin (1996). *Game of Thrones* premiered in the United States in 2011, and due to its phenomenal success, has been financed to run until 2018. It has received more awards than any other primetime scripted television series. It features scenes of sadistic and violent torture, rape, and murder in every episode. It captures and depicts the darker side of human behaviour, and judging by its popularity, the general public clearly has an appetite for this.

Throughout *Game of Thrones*, the heroes seem to have exchanged their virtue for sadism. Like the villians, they do their fair share of killing and betrayal and are equally brutal and sadistic in meting out justice and claiming victory. The villains, however, unlike the heroes, range from the supernatural to the psychotic. One example of this is the story involving the High Sparrow, the leader of the religious sect known as the Sparrows, and the treacherously scheming Queen Mother, Cersei. The High Sparrow is depicted as a morally upright, pious, harmless old man until it comes to enforcing moral beliefs that he equates with the will of the Gods. This is best illustrated in the story where he deviously imprisons Queen Cersei and then offers her the chance to atone for her sins in exchange for her release from captivity. Until she acquiesces, Queen Cersei is caged in his dungeons and treated pitilessly. Once she confesses to her sins of adultery, incest, and regicide, the High Sparrow suggests she perform the walk of atonement, a public ritual of punishment and penance. Queen Cersei then walks a certain distance as the Gods made her, that is, naked and with her glossy long hair brutally shorn, exposed to the hateful eyes and humiliating jeers of the mocking crowds that have gathered to shame and insult their despised Queen Mother.

Another dominant storyline running through the series revolves around Lord Ramsay Bolton, the legitimised bastard son of Lord Bolton and an unidentified wife of a miller. He is sent by his father to retake Winterfell (seat of the ruler of the North, and home of House Stark) from Theon Greyjoy. Ramsay takes Theon prisoner and tortures him brutally and mercilessly, eventually breaking him into being his pet called Reek. The dramatisation of the titillation of Theon, where two naked women sexually arouse Theon in preparation for his barbaric torture and gruesome castration is watched by Ramsay as well as the television viewers. As the plot develops, Ramsay sadistically lures and murders his father, his father's wife, and their new trueborn son, thus cementing his position as the new Warden of the North. Soon, however, he is defeated by members of House Stark and the scene in which his ex-wife Sansa Stark feeds him to his own hungry hounds is yet more evidence of sadistic violence that runs throughout this series, not that more evidence is needed by this point.

Through books, movies, computerised video games, and drama, the stories we are being sold as representing aspects of contemporary culture market two commodities: sadism and victory. How might we understand this? And can psychoanalysis help us make meaning from this aspect of human relating?

In the late nineteenth century, Krafft-Ebing (1898) introduced the term *sadism*, naming it after the French writer Comte Donatien François de Sade (1740–1814), also known as the Marquis de Sade, who described it in his novels, notably *Les 120 Journées de Sodome* (1795). Krafft-Ebing used the term to refer to sexual pleasure derived through the act of inflicting pain and suffering on others. In 1915, Freud, in one of his papers on metapsychology, "Instincts and their vicissitudes", defined sadism as exercising violence upon the other without any concomitant sexual pleasure. It is only in the masochistic phase that pain is accompanied by sexual excitation. Laplanche and Pontalis state that Freud believed sadism was prior to masochism, and that masochism is sadism turned round upon the subject's own self (Laplance & Pontalis, 1973). In other words, Freud suggested that sadists experienced sexual pleasure in causing pain when identified with the suffering object.

The experience of sexual arousal in response to stimuli like fetish objects, situations, fantasies, or individuals not typically associated with sexual behaviour is called paraphilia. It includes sexual practices that involve sadism and masochism. The American Psychiatric Association's *Diagnostic and Statistical Manual of Mental Disorders*, fifth edition (DSM-V) is the prevailing resource for diagnostic criteria of paraphilia. It describes sexual sadism as one in which patients report recurrent and intense sexual urges and fantasies where causing psychological or physical pain or suffering to another is sexually arousing to the self. However, there is debate over what constitutes unusual sexual interests and paraphilic ones. Some suggest that the focus should be on the effect of the sexual fantasy, rather than its content, thus tapping into the commonly held view that as long as sexual sadism is enacted with a consenting adult partner, it is not a psychological disorder (Joyal, 2014; Joyal et al., 2015). This perspective formed the basis for the *Fifty Shades* trilogy by British author E. L. James (2011) that topped best-seller lists around the world in 2015, was translated into fifty-two languages and adapted into a film by Universal Pictures in 2015.

Stories and images of sadomasochistic relating being presented to us as entertainment indicate there is a general appetite for, and popular fascination with, this kind of phenomenon. There is also unease about whether we regard it as a DSM-V classified illness or perversion, or whether we normalise it as something that is inherently present in every relationship.

One of the ways in which we might understand what is happening in the external world of popular culture is to pay closer attention to our internal worlds. Psychotherapy makes it possible to understand how these internal worlds influence how we relate in the external world. What happens in the consulting room can help us understand what is happening in the world outside. This is the premise on which this book is founded. It looks at the phenomenon of sadomasochism at different stages of the human life cycle: childhood, adolescence, adulthood, and in later life. The idea for this book germinated from a seminar series on "Working Psychotherapeutically with Sadism" that was held in central London from October to December 2014. The series provided psychotherapists who have specialised in this area an opportunity to think about the dynamics of sadism in their work with individuals and couples. This book offers another forum in which those psychotherapists, joined by some others, develop their thinking about patterns of sadism that emerge during clinical work and consider its developmental roots. It does not seek to provide an explanation or a theory of sadomasochism. Instead, it offers a thinking space in which we might further our understanding of the developmental roots of sadomasochistic relating and how this can manifest at different life stages.

The first two chapters explore sadism and violence in children and adolescents from the perspective of working psychotherapeutically with adolescents performing sadistic acts as well with those who have been the victims of sexual sadism.

In Chapter One, Graham Music deepens our understanding of sadism and violence perpetrated by children towards other children as well as towards adults (as in the case of child soldiers). Music is a forensic child and adolescent psychotherapist. Through clinical case illustrations of children exhibiting sadistic behaviour, he distinguishes between reactive sadism, where people respond to provocation by wanting to hurt, and proactive sadism, where sadistic acts are carried out in a cold and calculated manner. He illustrates how sadism in children who display a deep-rooted and immovable callousness can be understood within the context of claustro-agoraphobic anxieties, where they cannot bear either closeness to or separation from their objects. Music describes how these children can externalise such internal struggles by enacting these in their external relationships with real people. Music also discusses cases where children exhibit pleasurable addiction to, and sexual excitement from, inflicting pain, and contextualises why these children tend to re-offend.

In Chapter Two, Damian McCann discusses the emergence of sadistic traits in adolescence, and he presents his therapeutic work with a teenager who behaved sadistically towards his mother. McCann worked with this boy in a child and adolescent mental health service (CAMHS) department of the National Health Service (NHS). He describes how this case necessitated a multidisciplinary, interagency approach as it crossed over from CAMHS into forensic services. McCann examines how the intergenerational failure of containment within the adolescent's family contributed to the emergence of his sadistic behaviour towards his mother. He questions the effectiveness of treatment interventions in this case, as mother and son joined forces to defeat the therapeutic efforts to break the toxic link between the two of them.

In Chapter Three, Morit Heitzler describes her work as a somatic trauma therapist with a deeply traumatised young woman who, as a vulnerable adolescent, was one of several teenage girls who was groomed, subjugated, and sadistically tortured sexually by a gang of paedophiles. Heitzler says that such intense trauma is experienced, stored, and remembered in the body because, during the trauma, parts of the brain involved in thinking and making sense of experience shut down. She demonstrates how somatic trauma therapies can help access the raw emotions lodged in the body which might otherwise remain unavailable to cognitive and verbal expression.

Valerie Sinason presents an account, in Chapter Four, of the dilemma of the perpetrator in sexual sadism. Sinason invites us to look closely at the world of ritual perpetrators in organised crime, differentiating between spiritual and ritual abuse, yet highlighting how both are united in using sadistic practices to cause pain, distress, and humiliation to their victims. She describes the difficulty of working therapeutically with perpetrators of sadism where the therapist can become a helpless participant in sadistic enactments. Sinason explains her work with people with dissociative identity disorder and closes by discussing the perpetrator's unbearable dilemma and society's response to it.

Developing the theme of adult perpetrators of crime involving sexual sadism, Richard Curen describes in Chapter Five his work as a forensic disability psychotherapist working with two middle-aged men with intellectual disability. Forensic disability psychotherapy does not condone crime but focuses on illness and risk, and treatment is based upon psychodynamic understanding of offending behaviour. Each of the two men Curen worked with presented with perverse sadistic preoccupations which they compulsively enacted as a way of controlling and manipulating others in their environment. Curen describes the challenges of treating intellectually disabled adults in a way where they begin to feel able to let go of pathological ways of relating.

Chapters Six and Seven are geared towards thinking about sadism in adult couple relationships. In Chapter Six, Brett Kahr describes neurotic sexual sadism in the non-forensic population. He presents the wide range and variety of ways in which couples can use the marital bed for sadistic enactments of aggressive feelings arising from unspoken disappointments or resentments within the relationship. Kahr points out that such sadistic enactments can have a detrimental effect on a couple's relationship, especially if the partners otherwise relate in non-sadistic ways.

In Chapter Seven, Susan Irving presents two case studies of marriages in which partners unconsciously projected their vulnerable, dependent selves into each other and sadistically attacked them in the unconscious hope that this aspect of the self could be borne and gradually integrated into the self. Understanding these sadistic enactments formed the crux of therapeutic work.

In Chapter Eight, John Miller views sadomasochistic tendencies within the framework of the family through his work with individuals, and highlights the important role that good family relationships play in developing healthy forms of relating.

Sandra Evans describes her clinical work with the elderly in Chapter Nine. She presents a range of interactions that can take place in later life that involve some sadistic elements, and which risk going unnoticed or unacknowledged. This, she warns, can have harmful consequences, particularly if left unchallenged. Evans goes on to describe situations where the elderly can behave sadistically as a result of ageing, illness, and loneliness, but also where they can become vulnerable to sadistic attacks from their carers, especially when illness or dementia, for example, increases their vulnerability.

* * *

There are some common themes that run through the nine chapters of this book. A dominant theme is the link between sadomasochistic enactments and an internal struggle with vulnerability and dependency. Here, Glasser's (1979) description of the "core complex" phenomenon is drawn upon to help understand how difficulties in managing dependency needs can result in a wish to control ultimately the desired object. The "core complex" is a pre-oedipal phenomenon that belongs to the struggle within a two-person relationship (i.e., mother and infant), predating awareness of triangular three-person relationships. Glasser describes how the infant faces a conflict between an intense longing for intimate closeness with the mother, a wish to merge ultimately with her, and the fear that such a merger will result in an annihilation of the self. In response to this annihilation anxiety, and in the service of self-preservation, the infant mobilises aggression directed at the mother. The consequent withdrawal and wish to destroy the mother are accompanied by the converse fear, that of abandonment, producing a fundamental conflict that gives rise to the psychically disturbing circularity of the "core complex". Glasser distinguished between self-preservative and sadistic violence, the former being resorted to in order to eliminate the threat posed by the object, whereas the latter is used to gain control and pleasure by dominating and inflicting pain on the object. Re-enactments of sadistically violent acts can then be understood as ways in which individuals dominate the object in an attempt to triumph over helplessness that is unconsciously projected into the object, thus endeavouring to overcome early traumatic experiences of vulnerability and dependency.

This kind of enactment leads onto the other emergent theme in the book, that of a connection between sadism and masochism, that sadomasochistic relating is part of a wider whole whereby a sadist needs a masochist and vice versa. There is an interactive element to this kind of relating, and it is more visible in the chapters on couple relationships where what gets enacted in the actual couple relationship is a kind of internal object relating. This is seen in couples where both partners share an unconscious hatred and intolerance of their own vulnerability and dependency needs: one partner can unconsciously project vulnerability into the other, who carries and expresses this projection for both of them, whilst simultaneously projecting contempt and hostility for vulnerability into the other who receives and expresses this projection on behalf of both of them. Because it is a shared unconscious dynamic, the partners can switch roles, so vulnerability in one partner is met with contempt in the other and vice versa. The underlying shared unconscious developmental hope, then, is that through repetitive enactments this vulnerability can be withstood, understood, and made acceptable within the relationship.

Third, a distinction is drawn by each of the authors between the sexualisation of aggression, of sexual excitement in the sadistic act, and something not sexual but subjugating. Although sadomasochistic relating could be linked with sexuality, it may have nothing to do with sexual behavior and could find expression through the withholding of sex, for example. This brings up the question: at what point does the aggression needed for ordinary expression of sexuality morph into something different?

The contributors to this book have demonstrated that clinical work with individuals and couples creates the space we need to think about the developmental trajectories that give rise to sadomasochistic patterns of relating which we may recognise in ourselves and others. Stories that emerge within the consulting room deepen our understanding of what can lie behind the fascination that stories and images of sadomasochistic relating in contemporary culture can excite. When they are presented in the public domain as entertainment, it may be that part of the appeal lies not only in entertainment but also in the encounter, from a safe distance, with powerful internal anxieties stemming from different developmental experiences. Such entertainment, not limited to cinema but most likely true of all the arts, then might function for the viewer to contain the "projection of their most private and often unconscious terrors and longings" (Gabbard, 2001, p. 14), offering audiences the opportunity to master infantile anxieties associated with early developmental crises, through vicariously observing others trying out solutions on their own.

The study of sadism presents tremendous challenges to the practising clinician in terms of its detection and its impact. How do we differentiate between ordinary hatred and sadism? How do we know when sadism represents an unmitigated attack and when it becomes a plea for some sort of misguided relationality? Can we treat sadism successfully, and if so, how? These are merely some of the questions posed by the clinical contributors to this volume.

Sadism will be with us for a long time to come. Sadism may, perhaps, prove to be an essential component of human nature. Should that prove to be the case, we hope that the chapters contained herein may help to shed some light on our understanding of this complex and dangerous aspect of the human psyche.

References

Benioff, D., & Weiss, D. B. (Dirs) (2011–). *Game of Thrones*. Fantasy drama television series, premiered on Home Box Office (HBO) in the United States 17 April.

Carroll, D. S. (2011). *Victory over Victory: An Essay Studying our Personal and Cultural Compulsion in Pursuit of Victory, its Costs, and its Alternatives of Arrogance or Modesty*. Xlibris Corporation (USA).

Foss, S., & Bernth, P. (Prod.) (2007–2012). *The Killing*. Released by Danish National Television Channel 1, DR1.

Gabbard, G. O. (2001). Introduction. In: G. O. Gabbard (Ed.), *Psychoanalysis and Film* (pp. 1–16). London: Karnac.

James, E. L. (2011). *Fifty Shades: The Trilogy Series*. London: Vintage.

Joyal, C. C. (2014). How anomalous are paraphilic interests? *Archives of Sexual Behaviour, 43*: 1241–1243.

Joyal, C. C., Cossette, A., & Lapierre, V. (2015). What exactly is an unusual sexual fantasy? *Journal of Sexual Medicine, 12*: 328–340.

Krafft-Ebing, R. (1898). *Psychopathia Sexualis*. Stuttgart: Enke.

Laplanche, J., & Pontalis, J. B. (1985). *The Language of Psycho-Analysis*. London: Hogarth Press.

Madonna (1984). Like a virgin. Title track of the studio album *Like a Virgin*. Released on 12 November by Sire Records.

Martin, G. R. R. (1996). *A Game of Thrones*. New York: Bantam Books.

Tarantino, Q. (Dir.) (1992). *Reservoir Dogs*. Distributed by Miramax Films.

Tarantino, Q. (Dir.) (1994). *Pulp Fiction*. Distributed by Miramax Films.

Tarantino, Q. (Dir.) (1997). *Jackie Brown*. Distributed by Miramax Films.

Tarantino, Q. (Dir.) (2003–2004). *Kill Bill, Volumes 1 and 2*. Distributed by Miramax Films.

Tarantino, Q. (Dir.) (2012). *Django Unchained*. Distributed by Sony Pictures.

Tarantino, Q. (Dir.) (2015). *The Hateful Eight*. Distributed by The Weinstein Company.

CHAPTER ONE

Angels and devils: sadism and violence in children

Graham Music

In this chapter, I think about children who display sadistic behaviours, using the twin vertices of psychoanalysis and developmental science research, such as neurobiology and attachment theory.

Thinking about children having sadistic tendencies can stir controversy. Typically, either of two poles is taken. One is a tendency to see children as "angels", to always give them the benefit of the doubt, and to see the more hopeful, positive aspects of the personality. With this often comes a naïve belief that showing troubled children kindness and love will be enough. This, of course, is a form of turning a blind eye to something that can be too disturbing to face. On the other hand, such children can be seen as innately aggressive and destructive, almost as the devil incarnate, with no redeeming features or hope for change. I try to steer a course between these views.

An extreme case is the infamous murderer Mary Flora Bell. In 1968, a child herself, she strangled to death two little boys in Scotswood, an inner-city suburb of Newcastle upon Tyne. Before her eleventh birthday, she had strangled a four-year-old boy, Martin Brown, in a derelict house. A few months later, she strangled three-year-old Brian Howe in local wasteland. Chillingly, she returned to carve an "M" onto his stomach. She also reportedly took scissors and cut his hair off, scratched his

1

body, and mutilated his penis. It is hard to imagine what could lead a child to such behaviour. We do know that her mother was a prostitute and "gave" a pre-school Mary to men to be sexually abused. Maybe more importantly, her mother seemingly tried to kill Mary on several occasions. Mary was said to have "accidentally" fallen out of windows, and her mother was seen giving her sleeping pills which she said were sweets. Mary was clearly a victim of almost unthinkable hatred, torture, and sadism, but judge and jury also understandably saw her as having severe psychopathic tendencies and as being a massive danger to other children.

A more recent notorious case that raises similar questions was the murder of two-year-old James Bulger by ten-year-olds Jon Venables and Robert Thompson. Bulger had paint thrown in his eyes, he was kicked, stamped on, had stones and bricks thrown at him, an iron bar dropped on him, and batteries were reportedly pushed into his anus. He had ten skull fractures and forty-three major injuries, so many that the actual cause of death could not be ascertained. There was also evidence of a premeditated plan to seriously harm a child.

Their case has given rise to much controversy. The families of the murdering boys were indeed dysfunctional, with alcoholism, depression, neglect, aggression, and deprivation. Thompson's alcoholic depressed mother often left her seven children to fend for themselves, and reports suggest biting, hitting, and mutual torture similar to the kind described in William Golding's novel *Lord of the Flies* (1983). Venables was terrified of his often violent mother. Nonetheless, it was harder to explain why these two particular boys, as opposed to other victims of neglect and chaotic homes, perpetrated such shocking acts.

Psychotherapists cannot be helpful unless we step outside the twin poles of blame (that is, seeing such children as evil psychopaths) or of overly empathic understanding (that is, seeing them only as innocent victims). We need to face squarely what might be going on in the minds and emotional worlds of children who perpetrate such acts, as well as watch for possibilities of change. Such issues arose during my work as consultant child and adolescent psychotherapist at the Portman Clinic, London, where I saw Bill, an eight-year-old boy. Bill had been caught indulging in sexual play in the toilets with younger children. The staff group were divided: seeing him as already a callous and serial sex offender, some felt that he should be excluded from school permanently to safeguard other children; others were fond of him and felt sad about his life and experiences. Bill's mother had been a drug user who almost certainly prostituted herself, and his father was probably his mother's pimp. He was living with his aunt, following child protection proceedings. Although his appearance, academic work, and social skills had improved since he had been living with his aunt, he had been coming to school looking unkempt and dirty. There were some worries about the aunt, as she had a reputation for instability.

Bill's case raises many dilemmas typical of the forensic cases I have worked with. Bill could be aggressive and cruel, had few friends, and he seemed to enjoy making other children feel bad. Yet this behaviour had abated somewhat in recent months, and it was not clear why. Was this cruelty a way of getting rid of bad feelings that he could not bear; in other words, a classic form of unconscious projection of such feelings into another? He had indeed been treated cruelly and without concern, and had been left to fend for himself a lot. Was the lessening of his aggression a sign of feeling better as a result of better care? Or was he just becoming more sophisticated in his manipulations? Was his aggression mainly cold and calculated or more a reactive response to frustration? A big question was whether or not the positive and caring feelings that he evoked in adults should be trusted. For example, he enjoyed the attention of his learning support assistant and often snuggled into her. Was he ordinarily craving affection, or was this a form of overly sexualised contact masquerading as innocent affection-seeking in which she was yet another person he was using for his own ends? These and many other questions are typical of what needs unpicking in making sense of such children. In order to do this, some understanding of the very different forms of aggression and violence is needed, as is a good sense of developmental trajectories and what happens when things go wrong.

Developmental perspective

From birth, we are primed to learn to fit into our existing social or cultural group, speak its language, and learn its particular social or cultural rules, for example via imitative processes (Meltzoff, 2007). Awareness of other minds starts early. By about four months, infants can know they are the object of another's attention, showing coyness, for example (Reddy, 2000), and soon most have sufficient understanding of other minds to be able to "tease" in mutual enjoyment (Reddy, 2008). A crucial developmental window at about nine months allows much more sophisticated understandings of "other minds", as seen in "joint attention", "social referencing", and secondary intersubjectivity (Trevarthen & Hubley, 1978). With these skills come early empathic capacities, but only if infants receive experiences that we tend to take for granted. In particular, this includes what Meins (2002) has called "mind-mindedness", that is, an awareness of someone being responsive to and caring about our thoughts and feelings. This is so often missing in maltreated children who lack early experiences of attunement and do not develop empathy or care for others.

By around fourteen months of age, most children have an innate desire to help others. Tomasello (Warneken & Tomasello, 2009) found that in experimental situations when an adult has a tricky problem, such as fetching out-of-reach objects or opening a cupboard door with full hands, most toddlers were quick to help, spontaneously motivated by empathic concerns and disliking seeing wrongdoing (Vaish et al., 2009).

Indeed, babies as young as a few months old show preference for "kindly" as opposed to "nasty" puppets, or animated characters who either "help" or "hinder" another figure (Hamlin et al., 2007). Young babies appear to comprehend another's intention (e.g., to help or be nasty) by showing surprise when an innocent character approaches a seemingly nasty animated object but not on approaching the "good guy" (Kuhlmeier et al., 2003). Such experiments (Bloom, 2010) show that babies can distinguish pro-social and anti-social behaviours. Maybe more surprisingly, such babies also prefer puppets that punish the bad figures over puppets who are nice to the bad guys; in other words, they have a rudimentary sense of justice and a desire to see bad behaviour punished.

Yet early empathy and helpfulness depends on receiving attuned and mind-minded attention, containment (Bion, 1962), and good-enough parenting (Winnicott, 1996). By the end of their first year, children have built up considerable expectations of relationships based on past experiences, which includes whether or not other people are likely to be kind or helpful (Dweck, 2009). Maltreatment inhibits the capacity for empathy. Ordinarily, toddlers respond kindly to other toddlers' distress in nursery, but abused children generally can show little or no empathy or concern for another's distress, and indeed could be quite aggressive to such children (Main & George, 1985). Securely attached children, who have been sensitively attuned to, consistently show more empathy (Mikulincer et al., 2005); the circuits in the brain central to empathy turn off in the face of stress, fear, and trauma (Shirtcliff et al., 2009). Analogous with what neuroscientists and other researchers seem to be discovering about developmentally sensitive periods in general (Thomas & Johnson, 2008), I hypothesise that in many maltreated children an early window of opportunity is missed when they might have developed ordinary empathy and compassion.

Aggression: the impulsive, hot-blooded kind

Some children commit aggressive and sadistic acts in the heat of the moment. They feel provoked and react by wanting to hurt. This is different to "colder", more proactive kinds of aggression in which children and adults show more calculation. Proactive aggressors do not feel bad about their anger, whereas impulsive reactive types often do (Arsenio et al., 2009). Harry, a child I worked with, became furious on being accidentally hit by a soft toy in the playground, convinced this was done by another child "deliberately". Harry was quick to assume that people were being unfair. Retaliating vengefully and explosively, he got into many fights. Such impulsivity and an inability to tolerate frustration can be fuelled by early abuse and trauma, and can lead to aggression, violence, and indeed cruelty. Such people often have poor social skills and misread cues, perhaps seeing anger and aggression where others would not. This can be a variant of self-preservative aggression (Yakeley, 2009), in which the other is seen as a serious threat, even as life-threatening. Shame also often leads to swift reactivity.

When under threat, more primitive brain areas fire up and the prefrontal regions, central to emotional regulation, are less online, unlike in children with secure attachments who tend to be less impulsive and more emotionally regulated. Children who suffer violence and trauma often lack much empathy and mentalising capacity (Arsenio & Gold, 2006) and can believe that life is not just, let alone safe and consistent.

For reactive children and adults, the motivation (fairness or justice) is there but they misperceive the motivations of others and can very easily feel that they are "victims". Their physiological arousal, such as heart-rate, shallow breathing, or sweating, tends to be greater (Hubbard et al., 2010), their amygdalae firing more strongly in response to pictures containing violence or threat than the average person (Qiao et al., 2012). Reactive aggression is associated with lower attention spans and verbal ability. The worse the early experiences, such as physical aggression from parents, the greater the likelihood of reactive, impulsive forms of aggressive behaviour to others (Lansford et al., 2012), with neurobiological concomitants such as high amygdala reactivity (McLaughlin et al., 2014).

A clinical illustration: Shane

Shane, six, was in foster care, and was capable of great cruelty. He had a background of serious abuse and neglect. His mother had been drug-addicted and a victim of severe domestic violence, much of which Shane had witnessed, and she had abandoned him at the age of two. In the next couple of years, he changed placements several times.

At the point of referral, he was at risk of exclusion from school. He was violent with other children, had few friends, was a playground bully, and he struggled to control himself, concentrate, or learn. In my assessment, I felt an edge of threat from him, finding that I was breathing shallowly, as if bracing for something to happen. He stated that the toys in the box were "for girls", a sign of his fear of softness and vulnerability as well as his lack of capacity for symbolic play. An inordinate amount of time was spent playing football, which he always wanted to win, and then he would yelp triumphantly and look disdainfully in my direction. He would often coax me into believing that I might have a tiny moment of success, always at the last moment quashing my hopes and leaving me feeling tricked, betrayed, and stupid. Shane was clearly projecting something of his own cruel experiences into me. He had enough understanding of my thoughts and feelings to work out how to trick me, but such hypervigilant attention to the other is very different to empathy. Yet I felt Shane's coldness was defensive, not primary, and he conveyed a fear of closeness, but also some wish and hope for it.

I had to address him at a very basic level, trying to name emotions, but with feeling ("that made you very very cross"). In our all too frequent football games Didier Drogba and John Terry were his heroes, ruthless and triumphant figures with whom he identified. It was possible to momentarily wonder about the feelings of his alpha-male idols and their character traits. He allowed this briefly before asking "can we play properly now?" Moments of thought could rarely be tolerated, while it was important that I faced head-on his identification with aggressive and cruel figures.

Six months later, partly out of frustration, but also with hope that some shift was occurring, I began playing with toy animals in front of him. I took a baby pig and a crocodile, and he taped the crocodile's mouth with Sellotape. Yet in a few seconds the protection afforded by the tape was rendered useless as a series of killings of large and small animals took place, gleefully and triumphantly. Chilling as this was, it allowed me to talk about feelings and what was happening, which in turn enabled him to continue playing.

Tiny moments of hope were creeping in. In one session, mid football game, he momentarily hesitated. Normally, I would have missed the moment, but this time I asked where his mind was. He looked surprised and then said "I was thinking about my old school", hopefully a sign of the tiniest beginnings of a thinker who could think thoughts (Bion, 1962b). I said "Wow, Shane, you really are having thoughts, and we can get to know your thoughts". This led to him saying how he wished he was still at his old school and how he thought about it for "lots of time".

Some sessions later, he talked about how "bad" he had been, probably told to do so by his carer. Playfully, with his help, we gave a name to this "Cross Shane", and I tried to guess what Cross Shane was feeling when he got so angry in a recent incident. He said "you sound funny" but seemed to be visibly relieved at the idea that "Cross Shane" might not be all of Shane. I saw examples of him being less reactive. The end of his pencil kept breaking, something that would have made him very angry previously, but this time he said "OK, I can do it" as he determinedly sharpened it. Some belief that things could come right was forming. I said, "Well, it is not so bad, that's a new Shane, not Cross Shane". He said, "No, that's Boy Shane", and a new character had formed, who played a role in our therapy for the remaining time.

A few weeks later, in the midst of a football game, he turned the light on and I noticed a slight flicker of interest and asked him what he noticed, and he said "the colour". I said, "Isn't that amazing, the room seems to change colour when you turn the light on". He did it again and looked at me, and then said "the room goes sort of pink". I said, "Yes, the whole room seems to change, and what is so reeeeaally interesting is that Shane, you noticed it", echoing what seemed to be a seedling of aesthetic appreciation (Meltzer et al., 1988). He looked pleased, did it again, and said "it makes a sound". I said, "Wow, yes you have noticed the sound it makes when you turn the light on". Then he said "it's like a star", which I repeated and added how interesting it was when we noticed things. This is the kind of open-eyed curiosity which, for most lucky babies, comes online automatically with attuned attention and trust-inducing relationships. Shane did not receive this and had not experienced the safety and ease that comes with having a good internal object. Interestingly, at the end of this session, for the first time ever, he "helped" me to put away his things into the box, an important, if small, change, and both school and home were spotting other examples, such as offering to help clean something up that was spilt.

Shane never became the calmest or most loving boy but he started to change. As he began to develop some belief that the world could be safe, and that some people such as myself and his carer could be trusted, something had begun to soften in him. The developmental input, and his experience of a new but very ordinary interest in the world, allowed him to drop his guard somewhat and become less reactive, cruel, and sadistic. Shane's sadism had been primarily projective and defensive and lessened when he felt safer. Obviously, it reared its head still when under threat, but new personality traits were forming, presumably alongside new brain pathways and bodily systems that could be accessed when he felt safe enough.

Cold aggression

Unlike Shane, some children and adults show a colder, more proactive form of aggression, often in deliberate targeted ways to achieve definite goals for themselves. They might seemingly read minds and intentions well but show little fellow-feeling or empathy. Many who display proactive aggression can also respond reactively when they feel angry (Thornton et al., 2013). However, proactive aggressive acts are often very calculated, and such children, sometimes called "happy vicitimsers" (Smith et al., 2010), often feel positive about their violence.

Unlike the reactive children and adults who often cry out against unfairness, cold-headed aggressors care little about those they harm and lack remorse (Arsenio & Lemerise, 2010). The aggression perpetrated might include non-physical forms of aggression such as taunting, gossiping, and excluding others (Marsee & Frick, 2010). Colder forms of aggression are harder to treat, partly because perpetrators often have less desire to change and can be motivated by the gains from aggression.

As Arsenio (2006) suggests, many children who come from backgrounds where love, support, and empathy were not available come to believe that relationships are about power, control, domination, and getting what one wants. This is a more cynical take on life, arising from toxic adverse experiences which were not compensated for by sufficient good ones. Many such children display severe anti-social tendencies, impulsivity, and behavioural problems. The more extreme are labelled as having *callous-unemotional* traits (Viding et al., 2008).

Joe, a young boy I worked with, filled me with dread before each session. He displayed a calculating coldness and could engage in chilling violence. The pictures he drew were of mutilated bodies, death, gore, and torture. He showed evident enjoyment in this, and in real life had tortured pets. At school, pupils and staff felt uneasy around him. Joe came from a home where there was both terrible neglect and quite shocking abuse. In his infancy, he was reported to have been left on his own on a sodden mattress for days, and also sexually and physical abused. I am not sure if my therapy with Joe would have been successful, but his foster placement soon broke down and he was placed in a residential unit far from my clinic.

Often, such children show callous-unemotional signs from an early age and much continuity into adult life (Frick & White, 2008). Many adult psychopaths as children were anti-social, started fires, tortured pets, and showed cruelty. The presence of callous-unemotional traits in children, alongside conduct disorders, hugely increases the likelihood of serious offending, violent crime, and shorter periods between re-offending (Brandt et al., 1997). Interestingly, the cold-heartedness might be more than a metaphor. Research has shown that a low heart-rate in very young children is predictive of traits like lying and fearlessness, both being classic callous-unemotional traits (Dierckx et al., 2014).

The question of why someone becomes a callous-unemotional child or adult psychopath is riddled with controversy. Key questions are whether it is due to genes or to environmental triggers such as serious early deprivation and abuse. Some experts have suggested a significant genetic loading for callous-unemotional traits (Viding et al., 2008). Others, such as Gulhaugen (2012), a highly experienced researcher and clinician who works with high-security prisoners, found that most psychopaths have had childhoods marked by abuse, trauma, and neglect.

We are beginning to learn that something has gone awry with their emotional circuitry. Shamay-Tsoory (2010) is one of many researchers who has found deficits in empathy and in the orbital prefrontal cortex, and poor connectivity between prefrontal brain areas and the amygdala. Poorly functioning prefrontal brain areas are linked to impulsivity, lying, stealing, and cheating, and psychopathic traits as they grew up (Anderson et al., 2000). Low autonomic arousal and lack of fear in infancy is predictive of later behavioural problems (Baker et al., 2013).

Unlike impulsively aggressive children, those with callous-unemotional traits barely react to negative emotional words or distressing pictures, such as of children in distress (Kimonis et al., 2006). When shown pictures of violence or horrific injuries, they have low physiological arousal, for example less sweating and even breathing. Not surprisingly, the lower the reactivity in brain areas that register another's pain, such as the amygdala, the worse the psychopathic traits (Marsh et al., 2013), while prefrontal areas necessary for empathy are also less activated (Decety, 2013). Callous-unemotional children have minimal amygdala response in the face of fear, compared to most of us (Jones et al., 2009), and seem barely affected by another's pain (Lockwood et al., 2013). Many abused children I work with show high levels of fearlessness alongside impulsive traits, maybe stealing from or hurting others on a whim.

Twelve-year-old Mick was the older of two siblings, adopted at four from an alcohol- and substance-misusing, neglectful, and promiscuous mother and a violent father. He was probably abused by a paedophile ring. Excluded on his first week at school, he had a tough, steely side to him. His interactions with others were purely instrumental, based on what he could get, and he seemed to take pleasure in seeing others hurt and in pain. During his play, dolls were cut up, mutilated, and tortured to his evident enjoyment. While he was hypervigilant enough to be able to monitor me and others for any sign of danger, he seemed to have no interest in other people's minds and feelings, except to use these for his own ends.

It seemed unlikely that before adoption anyone would have shown interest in his thoughts or feelings. He was particularly cruel to his little sister. When I mentioned her in a session, his eyes went icy cold. At home, his parents reported finding him twisting her arm right back, squeezing her as hard as he could, showing no remorse when he hurt her.

Typically, in one early session he told me, smirking, that he had deliberately broken a child's leg. Therapeutically, it was important to show him that I could really bear and tolerate the depth of his cruelty.

Ironically, he described such violence as "therapy", because it made him feel better. When I suggested that this was a way of not bearing the feelings inside him, he parried this, telling me how he feels better if he gets revenge. He talked about how one needed to get back at people, saying "I have no choice". I questioned this, and he insisted that it was their fault. I said "if you feel bad it is always someone's fault?", and he said that "it is, isn't it?", clearly living in Klein's paranoid-schizoid position with an unshakeable conviction in the law of talion.

In time, there was the slightest hint that he was becoming able to admit to feelings of neediness and upset. He had struggled with a break in therapy. During this time, he was particularly unhappy but also nasty to those around him. I took up whether he could believe his vulnerability could be accepted and borne. He looked sad momentarily, and I commented on how hard it was to bear that he had a weak and dependent side. He almost took this in, appearing touched, and then squirmed out of this feeling, taking on a pseudo-strong posture a bit desperately. I said he seemed determined that we would not leave the room without me feeling just a bit of how desperate he felt, and he asked "well do you?", with some cynicism. But I thought his response contained at least the faintest touch of hope as well as sadism.

He was slowly taking back projections of weakness, of incompetence. In the next months, the sadism shifted in part to despair and even edged towards more depressive feelings. He began to notice and be interested in me in a way that was not hypervigilant, nor as manic or manipulative as before.

In the end, my therapy with Mick was not the most successful, in part because his foster placement broke down and he had to leave the area. However, progress had been slow and he had continued to manipulate and show little concern for other children as he remorselessly bullied them. He left just as some internal softness was beginning to form, and I will never know if this could have been built upon. Just as Alvarez (1992) and others have argued that, when working with autistic children, we have to find and help to grow the "non-autistic" parts of the personality, with callous-unemotional children like Mick, we have to try and find and make a relationship with non-callous, more hopeful aspects of the personality, however small and fragile.

Mick, typically, was on course for gaining a criminal record and had already been found stealing, bullying, causing serious injury and damage to property. We are not sure why some children experiencing terrible things are more likely to develop in this way than others (Viding et al., 2012). Yet any trip into a high-security prison reveals consistent tales of adults who were once like Mick, with early lives marked by abuse, neglect, trauma, and lack of basic parenting, as those who spend their professional lives working in these units attest to. It is almost unheard of to come across a violent or psychopathic criminal who has had a relatively ordinary childhood, and often the stories are unthinkably horrendous, as Gullhaugen's research backs up (2011, 2012).

Poor early attachment (Pasalich et al., 2012) and maltreatment (Kimonis et al., 2012) are linked to callous-unemotional traits, including in children adopted from neglectful orphanages (Kumsta et al., 2012). Several studies have found links between early trauma and psychopathy (Patrick et al., 2010; Poythress et al., 2006). Gullhaugen found that many psychopaths had parents who were uncaring and neglectful, and/or extremely rigid and controlling. This might explain some anomalies. Neglect, the absence of good experiences, might be more likely to lead to the kind of dampened-down lack of reactivity we see in psychopathy, but neglect is also harder to spot and research than overt trauma and abuse (Music, 2009). It is worth remembering that good parenting can reduce the risk of externalising behaviours in children with callous-unemotional presentations (Kochanska et al., 2013), and psychological treatment can be effective if given early enough (Hawes et al., 2014).

Core complex: a case example

Thirteen-year-old Sophia is typical of many Portman patients who seem at first glance to have a deep-rooted and immovable callousness. In fact, much of her anger and aggression was rooted in a desperate attempt to ward off unmanageable feelings, particularly of desperation, and both a fear of closeness and desperate urge for it. This has been described in terms of a claustro-agoraphobic syndrome (Rey & Magagna, 1994), in which patients can bear neither closeness nor separation from the object. A former director of the Portman Clinic, Glasser, conceptualised this in terms of the "core complex", seen frequently in sadistic and aggressive patients (Glasser, 1986, 1992). Glasser saw the "core complex" as a universal stage that all must go through, but I prefer to see it as a compromise formation in response to less than optimal early experiences.

A central feature of the "core complex" is the withdrawal from the object, which leads to a sense of desolation and aloneness. This can then become unbearable and in turn lead to clinging to the object, or in many patients, a need to take control and possession of it. The patient fears both aloneness and engulfment. A narcissistic and omnipotent psychic organisation can result, in which power and control is relied upon, often sexual power, rather than whole-object relating. Thus loneliness and abandonment are avoided via aggression and control, often sexualised, all in a desperate attempt to end the cycle seen in the "core complex". However, the cost is that any hope for real object relating gets lost. In such "core complex" defences, we see a denial that goodness comes from a source other than the self, and a disavowal of love and care from another.

Sophia came from a traumatised background and developed a "selfish" and unthinking approach to others. She was the youngest of four children, all of whom had different fathers. The atmosphere in the home was described as uncaring and cruel, although Sophia initially saw nothing unusual in it. Any weakness and vulnerability was met with taunting and vindictiveness from siblings and no sympathy from parents, who fought bitterly for much of her childhood before separating.

In early sessions, I found myself quite shocked by her descriptions of her relationships. She used sexual acts as a weapon, to wield power and hurt. She was in a relationship with a boy whom she physically hit and attacked, and was unfaithful to him, especially when she felt vulnerable. The chilling nature of her descriptions was slightly tempered by hints of her vulnerability. She described terrifying dreams of being attacked and chased and reported night terrors and fears of being left alone as a young child.

Despite my being old enough to be her grandfather, she was very seductive, and would, for example, explicitly state the attributes in older men she found attractive, and ask me to comment on her clothes. She seemed both disappointed and relieved when I could talk about her provocations and how she struggled against believing in a helpful, non-exploitative relationship, and she might feel triumphant if she destroyed this. Indeed, she attacked anything that could make her feel ordinarily cared for or at ease; she was more likely to attack her boyfriend, sexually humiliate him, or be unfaithful when she felt need of him, and she was both more seductive and dismissive of me when she had allowed herself to be touched by our work.

She described bullying and being controlling of peers too, and ruthlessly picked on traits in others that she denied in herself. Weakness was hated, despised, and projected into others, whether her boyfriend, her father, me, female friends, or other sexual partners. She manifested a classic example of Rosenfeld's internal mafia-like gangs (1987), viciously defending against vulnerability and weakness. She hated all softness, and interestingly could not sleep in an ordinary bed with pillows and a mattress, preferring the hardness of lying on the floor. She idealised strong and invulnerable characters, especially tough athletes who showed no emotion. My analytic stance of being more silent than she expected was partly viewed as a sign of my power, something she was rather enthralled by. She glorified in taunting and disparaging anyone who was in trouble or needed help. Sophia's lack of empathy was largely a desperate defence against her own vulnerability but also driven by anxious fear-ridden states of mind, which turn off empathy for others.

Slowly, though, she became interested in therapy, in me, and in herself. The initial signs were again in projected form, with her becoming fascinated by a woman who came out of a session into the waiting room streaming with tears each week. She could not understand how anyone could allow that to happen, but was also increasingly intrigued by the tissues in the room and who might use them. Slowly, I saw signs that she was taking in something more helpful and nourishing from statements like "maybe it is hard to believe that I can understand how that feels for you", or "perhaps myself and others might feel sympathy for what you are going through", comments that initially were met with disdainful looks but led to her showing fleeting signs of being touched.

She was forming a few better friendships and was in a more trusting sexual relationship, allowing herself to be somewhat dependent. Before a holiday break, she was able to describe her wish to retaliate, by, for example, leaving therapy, just as she threatened to be unfaithful in her relationship when her vulnerability was triggered. "Core complex" issues were starkly visible. Yet now she could allow herself to stay with her upset and worries, give up the idea that I was enjoying her weakness from a superior place, and even dare to describe hopes for her future.

She was beginning to have some compassion for herself, and for others. She was no longer disdainful of the "crying patient" who preceded her but seemed genuinely interested. She reported making small and generous gestures to others, such as offering to look after her oldest brother's children. In therapy, she noticed my states of mind, for example expressing concern when I had a cold, instead of the previous disdain. It seemed important that such gestures were accepted with ordinary gratitude. I do not claim that this work changed her from a tough, selfish individual to a kindly, empathic, altruistic one, but there were moves in that direction. The receptionist, who rarely commented on patients, said how she seemed softer, nicer, and I thought this too.

Addiction and sexual addiction

Unlike Sophie's more "core complex" reactivity, I have worked with many patients who exhibit pleasurable addictive, and sometimes sexual, excitement in inflicting pain. Many sadistic acts seem to be a way of managing, or at least avoiding, unbearable affects and so function as a form of anti-depressant. This makes sense in terms of their addictive quality. I think much compulsive and addictive behaviour starts for defensive reasons, perhaps as an attempt to manage "core complex" anxieties, stress, trauma, or inadequacy. However, such defences too often become addictive in their own right. Aggression and violence, sexual and non-sexual, can become addictive in similar ways to gambling, drugs, or pornography. For example, many soldiers in war-torn areas speak of the excitement and pleasure of killing, often called "appetitive violence" (Weierstall et al., 2013), with many perpetrators stating how their pleasure increases when they see spilled blood. Indeed, some soldiers return to a war zone because they miss the power and the thrills. Research with child soldiers in the Congo suggested that such a return to fighting actually warded off post-traumatic stress symptoms (Weierstall et al., 2012).

In compulsive sexual behaviours, similar brain pathways are triggered as in other forms of addiction (Voon et al., 2014), particularly in those areas involved in the dopaminergic system, such as the nucleus accumbens or ventral striatum (Kalivas & Volkow, 2014). Dopamine is the hormone central to seeking, including pleasure-seeking. Its function is to drive us towards things we need or want, such as food or sex, but it does not in itself provide the pleasure sought. People turn towards sexually compulsive behaviour, such as internet pornography, as an antidote to painful or unbearable affects, just as people turn towards a drug of choice, or alcohol or shopping (Music, 2014).

Thus perpetrators might resort to sexually abusive acts when they feel down, angry, or humiliated.

Many children and adults take pleasure in another's suffering. This probably has evolutionary significance: when people take too many resources or get too big for their boots, then we like to see them punished (for the good of the group). When such people fall from grace, we often experience *Schadenfreude*, that pleasure in another's downfall, and this causes reward circuits in the brain to fire up (Jankowski & Takahashi, 2014). Historically, people have taken pleasure in punishment and revenge, for example watching public executions or gladiatorial combats, or the pleasure expressed in a wish to "bomb them bastards" (Gilbert & Gilbert, 2015). In such processes, empathic brain circuitry gets turned off (Bhanji & Delgado, 2014) as the reward circuitry comes online.

In order to perpetrate sexual aggression, fellow-feeling for the victim needs to be obliterated. This requires a narcissistic, non-object-related state of mind. As Meloy (2007) has shown, in the psychopath we not only see low levels of anxiety and fear, but also a severely constricted affective world, low levels of emotional literacy, and poor capacities for attachment and object relating. As Meloy suggests, psychopaths tend to function at what we might think of as a pre-oedipal level, and certainly with little capacity for identification or internalisation, particularly of anything that might resemble a superego. They often identify with their aggressors, though, in the sense that Anna Freud (1972) described, as a way of managing feelings of humiliation.

Yet despite, or perhaps partly because of, such a poorly developed internal and emotional world, such perpetrators often experience a form of psychic deadness, as Gilligan (2009) and others have shown. It is no coincidence that patients at the Portman Clinic often re-offend at times of emotional stress or pain. Such patients struggle to process feelings and seek something that will compensate. Sexual violence and aggression thus can become a kind of anti-depressant, and an addictive one. This can be exacerbated if behaviours become entrenched patterns and then traits (Perry et al., 1995).

An eleven-year-old, Les, was caught forcing his nine-year-old brother to suck his penis. There was a long intergenerational history of sexual abuse and domestic violence. Relationships in this family were based on fear and asserting control and power. On our advice, social services removed Les, and he was placed in a residential unit. Here, though, he continued to be a risk to other children, particularly when something happened that would stir up difficult feelings, such as his key worker being away. Les had poor emotional vocabulary, little trust, and he treated most people with contempt. In therapy sessions, he was another child who loved to trick me and then smirk with disdainful pleasure. We learned not only about terrible violence towards his mother by her partners, but also historical acts perpetrated by Les himself, including molesting a four-year-old a few years back. Les seemed to be almost uncontrollably driven to act in this way. Given any access to the internet, he would be watching pornography. Yet, as I got to know him, I was struck by the paucity of his internal world, and of a mind that seemed empty and flat. It became apparent that the recourse to sexual stimulation, often at others' expense, was a way of feeling less dead and more excited. Until healthier ways of feeling real and emotionally alive could be developed, I feared that he would continue to behave as he did.

Sadistic sexual acts such as those perpetrated by Les are perhaps the ones that stir up the biggest anxieties. Like Les, a hugely disproportionate percentage of children who exhibit sadistic, sexually deviant behaviours have been victims of sexual offences themselves (Ogloff et al., 2012), and come from backgrounds high in conflict, neglect, and poor emotional care (Riser et al., 2013). In such cases, we see the lack of an experience of empathy and care, often experiences of overt cruelty, as well as excitement and pleasure in the aggressive and sexual acts. Such children and young people tend to have a view of the world, and of other people, as fundamentally untrustworthy and dangerous (De Ganck & Vanheule, 2015).

In adolescence, when the dopaminergic circuitry is fast developing (Blakemore & Mills, 2014), risks of addictive behaviours are heightened, whether to drugs, computer games, or sexual and other forms of cruelty and sadism. Often, what starts as an understandable defence, such as hurting another because one is feeling hurt, can transform into a behaviour that becomes pleasurable in its own right, and addictively so. In these instances, one has to focus on the underlying issues, but also on the addictive nature of the sadistic pleasure.

Summary

In this chapter, I have looked at sadistic behaviour in children, alongside violence, and focused on forms of psychic organisation seen in both reactive and more callous presentations. I have discussed the difficulty of facing up to the unpalatable fact that in some children we see what we would rather not believe, the brutal facts of genuine sadism and cruelty in children. A focus has been on how sadistic and aggressive acts can often be defensive, and projective, and attention has been given to the power of "core complex" anxieties. I have also discussed how behaviours that begin as defences against unbearable psychic experience can become not only character traits but also addictive, harnessing the same brain pathways as in other forms of addiction.

The chapter has described clinical case examples of sadism and aggression in cases where reactive aggression, callous-unemotional traits, or "core complex" anxieties have been at the fore. I have suggested that real change is possible, albeit incrementally, particularly in more reactive types, and especially when some trust and hope about the potential goodness in human relationships and the world can be facilitated.

References

Alvarez, A. (1992). *Live Company: Psychoanalytic Psychotherapy with Autistic, Borderline, Deprived and Abused Children*. London: Tavistock/Routledge.

Anderson, S. W., Damasio, H., Tranel, D., & Damasio, A. R. (2000). Long-term sequelae of prefrontal cortex damage acquired in early childhood. *Developmental Neuropsychology, 18*: 281–296.

Arsenio, W. F., Adams, E., & Gold, J. (2009). Social information processing, moral reasoning, and emotion attributions: relations with adolescents' reactive and proactive aggression. *Child Development, 80*: 1739–1755.

Arsenio, W. F., & Gold, J. (2006). The effects of social injustice and inequality on children's moral judgments and behavior: towards a theoretical model. *Cognitive Development, 21*: 388–400.

Arsenio, W. F., & Lemerise, E. A. (Eds.) (2010). *Emotions, Aggression, and Morality in Children: Bridging Development and Psychopathology*. Washington, DC: American Psychological Association.

Baker, E., Shelton, K. H., Baibazarova, E., Hay, D. F., & van Goozen, S. H. (2013). Low skin conductance activity in infancy predicts aggression in toddlers two years later. *Psychological Science, 24*: 1051–1056.

Bhanji, J. P., & Delgado, M. R. (2014). The social brain and reward: social information processing in the human striatum. *Interdisciplinary Review of Cognitive Science, 5*: 61–73.

Bion, W. R. (1962a). *Learning from Experience*. London: Heinemann.

Bion, W. R. (1962b). A theory of thinking. *Melanie Klein Today. Development Theory and Practice, 1*: 178–186.

Blakemore, S.-J., & Mills, K. L. (2014). Is adolescence a sensitive period for sociocultural processing? *Annual Review of Psychology, 65*: 187–207.

Bloom, P. (2014). *Just Babies*. New York: Crown.

Brandt, J. R., Kennedy, W. A., Patrick, C. J., & Curtin, J. J. (1997). Assessment of psychopathy in a population of incarcerated adolescent offenders. *Psychological Assessment, 9*: 429–435.

De Ganck, J., & Vanheule, S. (2015). "Bad boys don't cry": a thematic analysis of interpersonal dynamics in interview narratives of young offenders with psychopathic traits. *Frontiers in Psychology, 4*: 4–8.

Decety, J. S. L. (2013). Brain response to empathy-eliciting scenarios involving pain in incarcerated individuals with psychopathy. *JAMA Psychiatry*: 1–8.

Dweck, C. (2009). Forum. In: M. Tomasello (Ed.), *Why We Cooperate* (pp. 125–136). Cambridge, MA: MIT Press.

Dierckx, B., Kok, R., Tulen, J. H., Jaddoe, V. W., Hofman, A., Verhulst, F. C., Bakermans-Kranenburg, M. J., Ijzendoorn, M. H., & Tiemeier, H. (2014). A prospective study of heart rate and externalising behaviours in young children. *Journal of Child Psychological Psychiatry, 55*: 402–410.

Freud, A. (1972). Comments on aggression. *International Journal of Psychoanalysis, 53*: 163–171.

Frick, P. J., & White, S. F. (2008). Research review: the importance of callous-unemotional traits for developmental models of aggressive and antisocial behavior. *Journal of Child Psychological Psychiatry, 49*: 359–375.

Gilbert, P., & Gilbert, H. (2015). Cruelty, evolution, and religion: the challenge for the new spiritualities. In: T. G. Plante (Ed.), *The Psychology of Compassion and Cruelty: Understanding the Emotional, Spiritual and Religious Influences* (pp. 1–15). Oxford: Praeger.

Gilligan, J. (2009). Sex, gender and violence: Estela Welldon's contribution to our understanding of the psychopathology of violence. *British Journal of Psychotherapy, 25*: 239–256.

Glasser, M. (1986). Identification and its vicissitudes as observed in the perversions. *International Journal of Psychoanalysis, 67*: 9–17.

Glasser, M. (1992). Problems in the psychoanalysis of certain narcissistic disorders. *International Journal of Psychoanalysis, 73*: 493–503.

Golding, W. (1983). *Lord of the Flies*. London: Penguin.

Gullhaugen, A. S. (2012). Redefining psychopathy? Is there a need for a reformulation of the concept, assessment and treatment of psychopathic traits? PhD thesis. Norwegian University of Science and Technology, Department of Psychology, Trondheim, Norway.

Gullhaugen, A. S., & Nøttestad, J. A. (2011). Looking for the Hannibal behind the Cannibal: current status of case research. *International Journal of Offender Therapy and Comparative Criminology, 55*: 350–369.

Gullhaugen, A. S., & Nøttestad, J. A. (2012). Under the surface: the dynamic interpersonal and affective world of psychopathic high-security and detention prisoners. *International Journal of Offender Therapy and Comparative Criminology, 56*: 917–936.

Hamlin, J. K., Wynn, K., & Bloom, P. (2007). Social evaluation by preverbal infants. *Nature, 450*: 557–559.

Hawes, D. J., Price, M. J., & Dadds, M. R. (2014). Callous-unemotional traits and the treatment of conduct problems in childhood and adolescence: a comprehensive review. *Clinical Child and Family Psychology Review, 17*: 248–267.

Hubbard, J. A., McAuliffe, M. D., Morrow, M. T., & Romano, L. J. (2010). Reactive and proactive aggression in childhood and adolescence: precursors, outcomes, processes, experiences, and measurement. *Journal of Personality, 78*: 95–118.

Jankowski, K. F., & Takahashi, H. (2014). Cognitive neuroscience of social emotions and implications for psychopathology: examining embarrassment, guilt, envy, and Schadenfreude. *Psychiatry and Clinical Neuroscience, 68*: 319–336.

Jones, A., Laurens, K., Herba, C., Barker, G., & Viding, E. (2009). Amygdala hypoactivity to fearful faces in boys with conduct problems and callous-unemotional traits. *American Journal of Psychiatry, 166*: 95–102.

Kalivas, P. W., & Volkow, N. D. (2014). The neural basis of addiction: a pathology of motivation and choice. *American Journal of Psychiatry, 162*: 1403–1413.

Kimonis, E. R., Cross, B., Howard, A., & Donoghue, K. (2012). Maternal care, maltreatment and callous-unemotional traits among urban male juvenile offenders. *Journal of Youth and Adolescence, 42*: 1–13.

Kimonis, E. R., Frick, P. J., Fazekas, H., & Loney, B. R. (2006). Psychopathy, aggression, and the processing of emotional stimuli in non-referred girls and boys. *Behavioural Sciences and the Law, 24*: 21–37.

Kochanska, G., Kim, S., Boldt, L. J., & Yoon, J. E. (2013). Children's callous-unemotional traits moderate links between their positive relationships with parents at preschool age and externalizing behavior problems at early school age. *Journal of Child Psychology and Psychiatry, 54*: 1251–1260.

Kuhlmeier, V., Wynn, K., & Bloom, P. (2003). Attribution of dispositional states by 12-month-olds. *Psychological Science, 14*: 402–408.

Kumsta, R., Sonuga-Barke, E., & Rutter, M. (2012). Adolescent callous–unemotional traits and conduct disorder in adoptees exposed to severe early deprivation. *British Journal of Psychiatry, 200*: 197–201.

Lansford, J. E., Wager, L. B., Bates, J. E., Pettit, G. S., & Dodge, K. A. (2012). Forms of spanking and children's externalizing behaviors. *Family Relationships, 61*: 224–236.

Lockwood, P. L., Sebastian, C. L., McCrory, E. J., Hyde, Z. H., Gu, X., De Brito, S. A., & Viding, E. (2013). Association of callous traits with reduced neural responses to others' pain in children with conduct problems. *Current Biology, 23*: 901–905.

Main, M., & George, C. (1985). Responses of abused and disadvantaged toddlers to distress in agemates: a study in the day care setting. *Developmental Psychology, 21*: 407–412.

Marsee, M. A., & Frick, P. J. (2010). Callous-unemotional traits and aggression in youth. In: W. F. Arsenio & E. A. Lemerise (Eds.), *Emotions, Aggression, and Morality in Children: Bridging Development and Psychopathology* (pp. 137–156). Washington, DC: American Psychological Association.

Marsh, A. A., Finger, E. C., Fowler, K. A., Adalio, C. J., Jurkowitz, I. T. N., Schechter, J. C., Pine, D. S., Decety, J., & Blair, R. J. R. (2013). Empathic responsiveness in amygdala and anterior cingulate cortex in youths with psychopathic traits. *Journal of Child Psychological Psychiatry, 54*: 900–910.

McLaughlin, K. A., Sheridan, M. A., Alves, S., & Mendes, W. B. (2014). Child maltreatment and autonomic nervous system reactivity: identifying dysregulated stress reactivity patterns by using the biopsychosocial model of challenge and threat. *Psychosomatic Medicine, 76*: 538–546.

Meins, E., Fernyhough, C., Wainwright, R., Gupta, M. D., Fradley, E., & Tuckey, M. (2002). Maternal mind-mindedness and attachment security as predictors of theory of mind understanding. *Child Development, 73*: 1715–1726.

Meloy, J. R., & Shiva, A. (2007). A psychoanalytic view of the psychopath. In: A. Felthous & H. Sab (Eds.), *The International Handbook of Psychopathic Disorders and the Law* (pp. 335–346). Sussex: Wiley.

Meltzer, D., & Williams, M. H. (1988). *The Apprehension of Beauty: The Role of Aesthetic Conflict in Development, Violence and Art*. Perthshire: Clunie Press for the Roland Harris Trust.

Meltzoff, A. N. (2007). "Like me": a foundation for social cognition. *Developmental Science, 10*: 126–134.

Mikulincer, M., Shaver, P. R., Gillath, O., & Nitzberg, R. A. (2005). Attachment, caregiving, and altruism: boosting attachment security increases compassion and helping. *Journal of Personality and Social Psychology, 89*: 817–839.

Music, G. (2009). Neglecting neglect: some thoughts about children who have lacked good input, and are "undrawn" and "unenjoyed". *Journal of Child Psychotherapy, 35*: 142–156.

Music, G. (2014). *The Good Life: Wellbeing and the New Science of Altruism, Selfishness and Immorality*. London: Routledge.

Ogloff, J. R., Cutajar, M. C., Mann, E., Mullen, P., Wei, F. T. Y., Hassan, H. A. B., & Yih, T. H. (2012). Child sexual abuse and subsequent offending and victimisation: a 45-year follow-up study. *Trends and Issues Crime Criminology and Justice, 440*: 1836–2206.

Pasalich, D. S., Dadds, M. R., Hawes, D. J., & Brennan, J. (2012). Attachment and callous-unemotional traits in children with early-onset conduct problems. *Journal of Child Psychology and Psychiatry, 53*: 838–845.

Patrick, C. J., Fowles, D. C., & Krueger, R. F. (2010). Triarchic conceptualization of psychopathy: developmental origins of disinhibition, boldness, and meanness. *Developmental Psychopathology, 21*: 913–938.

Perry, B. D., Pollard, R. A., Blakley, T. L., Baker, W. L., & Vigilante, D. (1995). Childhood trauma, the neurobiology of adaptation, and use-dependent development of the brain: how states become traits. *Infant Mental Health Journal, 16*: 271–291.

Poythress, N. G., Skeem, J. L., & Lilienfeld, S. O. (2006). Associations among early abuse, dissociation, and psychopathy in an offender sample. *Journal of Abnormal Psychology, 115*: 288–297.

Qiao, Y., Xie, B., & Du, X. (2012). Abnormal response to emotional stimulus in male adolescents with violent behavior in China. *European Child and Adolescent Psychiatry, 21*: 193–198.

Reddy, V. (2000). Coyness in early infancy. *Developmental Science, 3*: 186–192.

Reddy, V. (2008). *How Infants Know Minds*. Cambridge, MA: Harvard University Press.

Rey, H., & Magagna, J. E. (1994). *Universals of Psychoanalysis in the Treatment of Psychotic and Borderline States: Factors of Space–Time and Language*. New York: Free Association Books.

Riser, D. K., Pegram, S. E., & Farley, J. P. (2013). Adolescent and young adult male sex offenders: understanding the role of recidivism. *Journal of Child Sexual Abuse, 22*: 9–31.

Rosenfeld, H. A. (1987). *Impasse and Interpretation: Therapeutic and Anti-Therapeutic Factors in the Psycho-Analytic Treatment of Psychotic, Borderline, and Neurotic Patients*. Oxford: Routledge.

Shamay-Tsoory, S. G., Harari, H., Aharon-Peretz, J., & Levkovitz, Y. (2010). The role of the orbitofrontal cortex in affective theory of mind deficits in criminal offenders with psychopathic tendencies. *Cortex, Journal Devoted to the Study of the Nervous System and Behaviour, 46*: 668–677.

Shirtcliff, E. A., Vitacco, M. J., Graf, A. R., Gostisha, A. J., Merz, J. L., & Zahn Waxler, C. (2009). Neurobiology of empathy and callousness: implications for the development of antisocial behavior. *Behavioural Science and the Law, 27*: 137–171.

Smith, C. E., Chen, D., & Harris, P. (2010). When the happy victimizer says sorry: children's understanding of apology and emotion. *British Journal of Developmental Psychology, 28*: 727–746.

Thomas, M. S. C., & Johnson, M. H. (2008). New advances in understanding sensitive periods in brain development. *Current Directions in Psychological Science, 17*: 1–5.

Thornton, L. C., Frick, P. J., Crapanzano, A. M., & Terranova, A. M. (2013). The incremental utility of callous-unemotional traits and conduct problems in predicting aggression and bullying in a community sample of boys and girls. *Psychological Assessment, 25*: 366–378.

Trevarthen, C., & Hubley, P. (1978). Secondary intersubjectivity: confidence, confiding and acts of meaning in the first year. *Language*: 183–229.

Vaish, A., Carpenter, M., & Tomasello, M. (2009). Sympathy through affective perspective taking and its relation to prosocial behavior in toddlers. *Developmental Psychology, 45*: 534–543.

Viding, E., Fontaine, N. M., & McCrory, E. J. (2012). Antisocial behaviour in children with and without callous-unemotional traits. *Journal of the Royal Society of Medicine, 105*: 195–200.

Viding, E., Jones, A. P., Paul, J. F., Moffitt, T. E., & Plomin, R. (2008). Heritability of antisocial behaviour at nine: do callous-unemotional traits matter? *Developmental Science, 11*: 17–22.

Voon, V., Mole, T. B., Banca, P., Porter, L., Morris, L., Mitchell, S., Lapa, T. R., Karr, J., Harrison, N. A., & Potenza, M. N. (2014). Neural correlates of sexual cue reactivity in individuals with and without compulsive sexual behaviours. *PLoS ONE 9*. http://dx.doi.org/10.1371/journal.pone.0102419.

Warneken, F., & Tomasello, M. (2009). Varieties of altruism in children and chimpanzees. *Trends in Cognitive Science, 13*: 397–402.

Weierstall, R., Schalinski, I., Crombach, A., Hecker, T., & Elbert, T. (2012). When combat prevents PTSD symptoms—results from a survey with former child soldiers in Northern Uganda. *BMC Psychiatry, 12*: 1–8.

Weierstall, R., Schauer, M., & Elbert, T. (2013). An appetite for aggression. *Scientific American Mind, 24*: 46–49.

Winnicott, D. W. (1996). *The Maturational Processes and the Facilitating Environment: Studies in the Theory of Emotional Development*. London: Karnac.

Yakeley, J. (2009). *Working with Violence: A Contemporary Psychoanalytic Approach*. London: Palgrave Macmillan.

CHAPTER TWO

Disturbed adolescence and the emergence of sadistic traits

Damian McCann

Introduction

Adolescence is generally regarded as a time of transformation, involving physical, emotional, and psychological change. For some young people, the risks associated with the transition are mitigated by the presence of, for example: self-esteem, having secure and affectionate relationships, good parental modelling, and the ability to process events and experiences in a meaningful way (Rutter, 1985). For others, however, the absence of a secure base, a history of violence, abuse, and neglect within the family, exposes them to a world of relationships that feel threatening and that then have to be conquered rather than embraced.

In this chapter, I will examine my attempted intervention with a particular adolescent who presented for treatment, mainly at the behest of his mother who was struggling to cope with his challenging and abusive behavior. The intervention posed particular questions concerning diagnosis, availability for treatment, and the emergence of a sadomasochistic relationship between mother and son. The work also raised questions concerning multidisciplinary and interagency work, as well as the interface between generic child and adolescent mental health services and the forensic services, which, according to Mullen (2000), represent a specialised area of criminality that involves the assessment and treatment of those who are both mentally disordered and whose behaviour has led, or could lead, to offending and acting-out. Drawing on psychoanalytic thinking, attachment theory, and concepts originating from the field of couple psychoanalytic psychotherapy, I hope to provide a window into the workings of the disturbed adolescent mind as well as the enmeshed mother–son dyad that essentially conspired to defeat all efforts to reach and effect change.

Sadism

Sadism, a term originally introduced by Krafft-Ebing in the late nineteenth century, referred to sexual pleasure derived through the act of inflicting pain and suffering on others (Krafft-Ebing, 1898). Since then, the term has been expanded to include non-sexual enjoyment derived from sadistic acts, and indeed Freud believed that sadism encompassed two separate disorders: sexual sadism and generalised sadistic behaviour (Freud, 1905d).

Sadistic individuals are believed to have poor locus of internal control, often manifested by outbursts of temper, irritability, low frustration tolerance, and a somewhat controlling nature. From an interpersonal standpoint, they are noted to be harsh, hostile, manipulative, lacking in empathy, cold-hearted, and abrasive to those they deem to be their inferiors (Myers et al., 2006). However, one might view this presentation more as an extreme form of defence against an absence of real power and control and a fear of complete psychic breakdown. Motz (2014) makes the point that sadism can be used defensively to enable someone who feels vulnerable to escape from an awareness of unpleasant feelings of being helpless and humiliated. Attention has also been drawn to the cognitive nature of such individuals exhibiting rigidity, social intolerance, and a fascination with weapons, war, and infamous crimes. With this profile, it is hardly surprising that sadists are often drawn to social positions that enable them to exercise their need to control others and to mete out harsh punishment or humiliation. In many respects, those exhibiting sadistic tendencies use physical cruelty or violence for the purpose of establishing dominance within an interpersonal relationship and the individual concerned might also take some pleasure in the psychological or physical suffering of others (including cruelty to animals).

There has been much debate within the field of psychiatry concerning the nature and diagnosis of sadism, with some locating it firmly within the realm of a personality disorder. According to the UK National Institute for Health and Care Excellence (NICE), conduct disorders and associated anti-social behaviours are the most common mental and behavioural problems in children and young people: "Conduct disorders are characterized by repetitive and persistent patterns of antisocial, aggressive and defiant behavior that amounts to significant and persistent violations of age appropriate social expectations" (NICE, 2014). The World Health Organization's International Classification of Diseases, Tenth Revision (ICD-10, 2005) further divides conduct disorders into socialised conduct disorder, un-socialised conduct disorder, conduct disorders confined to the family context, and oppositional defiant disorder. The major distinction between oppositional defiant disorders (defined by the presence of markedly defiant, disobedient, and provocative behaviour) and the other sub-types of conduct disorder (involving dissocial and aggressive acts that violate the law or the rights of others) is the extent and severity of the antisocial behaviour. Isolated or antisocial acts are not sufficient to support a diagnosis of conduct disorder or oppositional defiant disorder. Oppositional defiant disorder is believed to be more common in children aged ten years or younger, whilst the other subtypes of conduct disorder are most evident in those aged eleven years or older. Conduct disorders in childhood are also associated with significantly increased rates of mental health problems in adult life, including antisocial personality disorder with or without psychopathy. More recently, the concept of psychopathy has been extended to children and adolescents: antisocial youths with psychopathic traits have been shown to have a greater number, variety, and severity of conduct problems in forensic, mental health, and community samples (Salekin & Frick, 2005).

It is also worth bearing in mind that a diagnosis of conduct disorder is, according to NICE, also strongly associated with poor educational performance, social isolation, and, in adolescence, substance misuse and the possibility of increased contact with the criminal justice system. Comorbidity operates as a confounding factor in the diagnosis since, according to the American Academy of Child and Adolescent Psychiatry, almost half of those diagnosed with oppositional defiant disorder or conduct disorder are also diagnosed with attention deficit and hyperactivity disorder (ADHD). Adolescents living with ADHD and a coexisting conduct disorder, such as oppositional defiant disorder, are at higher risk for antisocial behaviour and suspension from school. The school dropout rate for this group is twelve times greater than the rate among adolescents who are not affected by ADHD; outcomes that underline the importance of early identification.

It has been suggested that parents of children living with ADHD and conduct disorder often feel frightened and intimidated by their child's behaviour and worry about danger or injury to other family members. Parents may also be shocked or embarrassed by their child's sadistic behaviours. At one and the same time, family members can act in ways that either reinforce or diminish the patient's problematic behaviour or thoughts, so their involvement is helpful and often essential. This is particularly evident in the clinical material relating to Marcus and his mother Rhona—a composite case example incorporating aspects of clinical work drawn from a range of clients seen over a number of years in several child and adolescent mental health services based in the Home Counties. All information relating to the clients has been changed to protect their confidentiality.

Clinical case

Initial meeting

Marcus, a fourteen-year-old boy, and his mother, Rhona, were being seen by the consultant child and adolescent psychiatrist. Marcus had been referred by his school to the child and adolescent mental health service because of concerns about his ability to concentrate and the ensuing extreme disruptive behaviour in class. Over time, the consultant psychiatrist found that he was struggling to manage the somewhat abusive nature of the relationship between mother and son, and because of this he felt it necessary to involve a family therapist, myself, to potentially help mediate the problematic dynamic. A meeting was arranged between Marcus, his mother Rhona, the psychiatrist, and myself. No sooner had the four of us sat down than Marcus began to verbally abuse Rhona by firing strongly worded expletives towards her in a raised voice. Marcus seemed to be driven by a pressing need for her to admit to the emotional and physical abuse she had perpetrated towards him as he was growing up. Her failure to make such an acknowledgement only served to exacerbate his efforts to make her account for her deeds and, through this uncomfortable exchange, she began to claim her status as a victim in the face of her son's attack. Interpreting the level of distress, together with attempts to create a space to think, had little effect in the ensuing battle between victim and perpetrator. In order to slow the pace, I drew on mentalization-based techniques, such as actively interrupting and insisting that mother and son each take turns in speaking. This helped to a limited extent in stemming the flow of the exchanges. However, Marcus felt that his mother was side-stepping the central issue, and he also became annoyed with our more active stance. In response to this, he donned his headphones and successfully managed to shut us all out. This then had the effect of creating an increased space for Rhona to express her concerns about her son's abusive behaviour towards her, and before long we were on the receiving end of a demanding and denigrating presence as Rhona accused us of failing to get to grips with a son who, from her point of view, was becoming an abuser. Faced with this scenario, my colleague and I managed to interrupt Rhona's diatribe and also successfully convinced Marcus that he needed to remove his headphones in order that we could offer our own reflections. Summarising the nature of the mother–son dynamic, we put forward the suggestion that we could offer each of them an individual space to think with one of us about their situation as a way of deciding how best to proceed. To our surprise, they both accepted this idea, and it was agreed that I would work with Marcus, whilst my colleague met with Rhona.

Background history

Marcus was of mixed race and the only child of Rhona and Mohammad, a lorry driver from Wales. Rhona met Mohammad having recently returned from her family home in Scotland, to where she had retreated after the breakdown of her previous marriage. Apparently, whilst living in London, her ex-husband had physically attacked her and she had escaped to a refuge, from where she had decided to return to Scotland to be nearer other family members. Once back there, she had struggled to adjust and had also managed to alienate those around her. Feeling alone, angry, and dissatisfied, Rhona made her way back south and secured a job working in a bar, which helped her re-establish a base. This is when she met Mohammad. Rhona believed that Mohammad offered her the possibility of love and security. She became pregnant with Marcus and for a time all seemed well. However, Rhona struggled with the transition to parenthood and also became angry and demanding of Mohammad, who by all accounts was on the road for long periods of time and who was often away overnight. Rhona became increasingly unsettled and the couple argued incessantly. Eventually, their relationship ended, and Mohammad left the family home when Marcus was two years old. Contact between Marcus and his father was irregular and sporadic. Following Mohammad's departure, Rhona's struggles intensified, as she contemplated a future on her own with a vulnerable and dependent two-year-old. Rhona's survival instincts helped her secure a new position as a shop assistant, and for a time things again seemed to settle.

Nevertheless, when feeling under pressure, Rhona was prone to regular outbursts of anger and rage, traits that seemed consistent with borderline states. Borderline personality disorder (BPD) is characterised by a pattern of intense and stormy relationships, uncontrollable anger, poor impulse control, affective instability, identity and cognitive disturbances, and recurrent suicidal behaviour. Even if Rhona does not quite fit this profile, it is safe to assume that Marcus was on the receiving end of his mother's rages on a regular basis. It has been suggested, perhaps not surprisingly, that children and adolescents of mothers with borderline personality disorder are at increased risk of developing psychopathology. For instance, in one study, adolescents aged eleven to eighteen years whose mothers had borderline personality disorder exhibited more attention problems, delinquency, and aggression than adolescents whose mothers had no psychiatric disorders (Barnow et al., 2006).

Individual sessions

Marcus was early for his first appointment with me. When I went to collect him from the waiting room, I found him pacing in the reception area. On seeing me, he rushed forward and accused me of being late. I guided him to the room and glanced at the clock to ensure that I had collected him at the agreed hour (I had). In an aggressive and somewhat menacing manner, Marcus told me that the clock was wrong and that it was unprofessional to keep people waiting. I said that if we could leave the issue of the clock to one side for the minute, it would be helpful to hear what he was feeling about coming to see me today.

Marcus dismissively informed me it was a complete waste of his time coming to talk when the problem was his mother, and so "you should be seeing her not me". On further probing, Marcus explained that he felt that his mother was a waste of space and that she needed to admit what she had done to him in the past, otherwise he would really teach her a lesson. I wondered what this would achieve, and he told me that he would at least have the pleasure of seeing her suffer as she had made him suffer. We talked about the past, and he described how his mother would regularly "lose it", inflicting both physical and mental suffering on her son. I wondered if he had ever told anyone about this, and he said there was no point, no one would believe him, and, in any case, as far as he was concerned, people are a waste of space and he was better off on his own. I wondered if he might think that I too would be unreliable as he felt that I had kept him waiting. Marcus reprimanded me for my failure to admit the truth in being late, and it was clear that I was now being put in the same boat as his mother, and indeed everyone else who failed to see and experience things exactly as he saw and experienced them.

Throughout the first meeting, Marcus' attitude was one of contempt, and as the session continued I occasionally glimpsed the depth of his hatred. In addition, he exhibited a high degree of narcissistic omnipotence (Freud, 1914c), especially when talking about school. For instance, he took great delight in telling me that the teachers were useless, always getting things wrong, and how it was his job to humiliate them, "how else are they going to learn?". I wondered if Marcus felt that this was his own school of learning, namely humiliation and psychological torture, and that he was now giving others a taste of their own medicine? Marcus fell silent and then turned towards me saying, "Don't tell me what I am feeling, you have no fucking idea what I am feeling so don't think you do". I was initially quite perturbed by his outburst, but it helped me understand the extent of his defences. Bateman (2006), drawing on Rosen's distinction between thick- and thin-skinned narcissists, speaks of such individuals employing strategies to protect themselves against a perceived threat from others. In essence, thick-skinned narcissists are inaccessible and defensively aggressive (Bateman, 2006), and I feel that Marcus reacted as he did because he experienced me as being critical of him as well as posing a threat to his defences.

Changing tack, I wondered if Marcus knew what I was feeling, pointing out that he seemed to be putting me through my paces as I tried to get it right for him. He responded by saying, "no one can get it right, no one knows what I am feeling and no one will ever know". I suggested that I thought he might be anxious about being understood, since it seemed important for him to feel in control, and that he seemed to be saying that there is a price to be paid for giving up that control. Marcus told me that I was talking shit and that it just confirmed the fact that he was better off doing it for himself. This devaluation of my contribution fits perfectly with the object-destroying nature of thick-skinned narcissists whose sole purpose is to triumph over others as the destructive self gains in strength. However, this can be viewed as a defence against the loss of real contact linked to the breakdown in Rhona's early attachment to Marcus.

Taking up the theme of anger and the pleasure he seemed to get from the suffering of others, Marcus' tone took on somewhat grandiose proportions, as he told me about the fights he got into at school. He also described in some detail an incident when he attacked another boy who was pestering him for money. Although I asked Marcus to explain, he was vague in his recollection, but I felt convinced that this was yet another example of him feeling got at by someone who wanted something from him. It seems that this boy's need got under Marcus' skin, a rupture to the boundary between self and other; resulting in Marcus having to defend himself in the only way he knew, namely attacking the other with the idea of total annihilation. Even if nothing more than a fantasy, I began to gird my loins, as I came to understand that entering Marcus' world was potentially dangerous given his wish and need to punish and torture others, especially those who were in danger of getting close to him.

Over the course of our work together, I generally found it hard to engage Marcus in thinking about what was happening to him. For example, any reference to his father angered him greatly, and on one particular occasion when I persisted with my curiosity about this relationship, Marcus leapt from his seat, stormed out of the room, and left the building. When he returned the following week, he told me that if I mentioned his father again, he would walk out. I was mindful that this was exactly what his father had done to him, but realising the extent of his fragility and not wishing to lose him, I sat in silence waiting to see what Marcus would do next. The silence that ensued seemed to go on for ever, but was eventually broken by Marcus donning his headphones and singing out loud. In addition to blocking me out, I also felt controlled by Marcus, who was essentially preventing himself from having to think about painful issues that seemed to excite disturbance in him. I also felt that there was a tortured quality to the relationship he was forming with me, and I assumed that it was a version of the relationship that operated between him and his mother. However, it is also possible that Marcus was trying to protect me from his anger and murderous rage by taking this outside of the consulting room rather than expressing it within the session.

In discussion with my colleague, I learned that Rhona was using her individual sessions to express her concern about Marcus and the way that he was treating her. Rhona made particular mention of Marcus' disturbance following contact with his father, which confirmed my own feeling that Marcus longed for a strong male figure to contain both him and his mother. In the absence of this, Marcus took on the role of attempting to control others and because of this, not surprisingly, Rhona communicated a fear of her son, whom she felt was outside of her control. At the same time, Rhona complained that professionals had failed to really get to grips with Marcus and demanded that more be done to help him. I took these communications as further evidence that I was failing both to engage Marcus and to contain the situation for her through my work with him.

These concerns were subsequently realised when, just after the Easter break, Marcus physically attacked his mother. The details of the incident were slow to emerge and each of them had their own version: Rhona claimed that Marcus attacked her while she was trying to get him to school, whereas Marcus maintained that his mother was shouting and screaming when she could see that he was trying to sleep. In the ensuing argument, Marcus insisted that he was ill, and when Rhona refused to leave his room, he got out of bed and tried to physically remove her from his room. It appeared that in the fight, Rhone lost her balance and banged her head hard on the wooden floor as she fell. When she regained consciousness, she discovered that Marcus had gone, and worried about the split to her head, she called for an ambulance. Given the nature of the attack, Marcus, once he had returned home, was then interviewed by the police. In view of his age and the circumstances surrounding the attack, social care were asked to assess the risk for Marcus and his mother continuing to live together. In light of the fact that Marcus' father lived some distance away and was often on the road, and that there were no immediate relatives who could offer Marcus a home, a decision was made to place Marcus in respite care. When I saw him next, he was living in a temporary foster-care placement. Despite the changed circumstances and the additional travel involved in coming to see me, Marcus was on time and clearly wanted to speak.

I was struck by the pleasure he was feeling, in that his mother, from his point of view, had finally got what she deserved. He told me that he had the right to protect himself against a mother who was mad. Marcus also took delight in casting aspersions on social care, paying particular attention to the fact that rather than caring for him they were ruining his life. He was derisive of the foster parent's input into his life, accusing her of "only being in it for the money", and he seemed to be on a new crusade, namely that of getting back to his own home. He took particular delight in telling me that his mother also wanted him home and that it was only a matter of time. I questioned this course of action, given the seriousness of his attack on his mother, but Marcus dismissed my concerns and sarcastically pointed out that, unless he was provided with a flat of his own, there was no other option but for him to return home. I felt concerned, but subsequently heard from my colleague that Rhona was also desperately trying to get Marcus home so that they could carry on with their lives together.

Although we strongly advised against this on grounds of safety, Marcus returned home within the week. For me, this was the first real indication of the sadomasochistic fit in the relationship between Rhona and Marcus, and in my countertransference I felt angry and outraged that they could be allowed to subvert a plan that had been put in place to create a safety zone for both of them. I was also surprised that my colleagues in social care had been rendered impotent in their efforts to provide a safe and secure base for Marcus, and I felt that the professional system was in danger of becoming yet another faulty container for Marcus who, with Rhona's help, had managed to undermine and subvert the safety plan.

The nature of the sadomasochistic fit

In trying to understand the relationship between Marcus and Rhona, I will draw on Glasser's (1996) concept of the core complex, as it provides a particular understanding of the development of the sadomasochistic fit. Glasser believed that the core complex had its origins in normal developmental phenomena characterised by the infant's wish to merge with an idealised, omnipotent, gratifying mother as an early solution to anxieties of loss engendered by its own move towards separation and individuation. However, problems arise for the infant within this developmental process if the primary object is unavailable or narcissistically oriented to the extent that the child is used to meet the narcissistic needs of the primary caregiver. The core complex therefore describes a movement between a deep-seated longing for the most intimate closeness with the object, and at the same time a terrifying flight away from the object because the desired merger threatens to result in annihilation of the self. The ensuing oscillation encapsulated in the confused interplay of closeness-annihilation and distance-abandonment was most evident in the relationship between Rhona and Marcus at points when Marcus experienced Rhona as a threat to his very existence, and Rhona acutely experienced feelings of abandonment once Marcus was removed from her care. Glasser goes on to suggest that this threat of annihilation may be dealt with through either a defensive narcissistic withdrawal, in depression, arrogance, contempt, or an aggressive withdrawal from the engulfing object with the aim of destroying its very existence. Both situations, however, produce a loss of the desired object together with the terror of abandonment, a fundamental conflict that constitutes the psychically disturbing circular nature of the core complex. The aggression associated with the core complex is therefore designed to achieve mastery over the object rather than fostering a capacity for concern or intimacy. Glasser suggests that the corruption of reality to meet narcissistically driven needs works against any toleration of dependence, separateness, loss, and ambivalence, since these are all experienced as a threat to the self.

Glasser goes on to draw a distinction between what he terms "self-preservative violence" and that which he termed "sadistic violence". Self-preservative violence works towards eliminating the threat posed by the object by attacking and destroying its source, whereas sadistic violence is more concerned with gaining control and pleasure by dominating and inflicting pain on the object. However, it is possible that sadistic violence based on sadomasochistic object relating may break down into more dangerous self-preservative violence if the object continues to feel persecutory and psychically toxic.

Indeed, Motz's thinking concerning toxic coupling is helpful in shedding further light on how each of the two individuals are destructively dependent on the other, unconsciously allied in a perverse bond (2014).

Although Motz writes about adult couple relationships, I feel that her observations hold in regard to this mother–son dyad. Indeed, these toxic partnerships can also be understood in the context of Welldon's (2012) work on malignant bonding; she highlights the perverse enmeshed relationship in which abuse and cruelty become the norm. Welldon sees violence within such relationships as the way in which partners attempt to overcome earlier trauma, that is, through re-enacting experiences in order to triumph over the helplessness. To me, Marcus was certainly engaged in an enactment in which he successfully projected his own helplessness into his mother whilst he triumphantly took on the role of the abuser determined to kill off the threatening and damaging object. One can only assume that Rhona's determination to have Marcus back speaks to her guilt and dependence, as well as her own masochism that finds a natural lock with Marcus' emerging sadistic wishes and behaviour. According to Motz, projection and projective identification are defences that keep these relationships alive and serve important functions, which, whilst ultimately destructive, are temporarily enlivening and addictive. Steiner (1993) also highlights the emergence of sadomasochistic-type relating, suggesting that love and hate function perversely since the phantasies encapsulated within the sadomasochistic relationship itself provide excitement and pleasure from cruelty, which is not inhibited by any recognition of hurt or damage to the object. The confusion and excitement that seem to characterise the relationship between Marcus and Rhona suggests a difficulty in linking hurt and pain in the meeting between subject and object, thereby preventing any kind of a "working through".

Although Rhona and Marcus were reunited, I was struck by the fragility of their attachment bond. Marcus had been desperate for an understanding mother, one who would offer containment for his more disturbed feelings and psychic pain. Rhona, however, was unable to provide this, as her own experience of being mothered was neither containing nor secure, and so there was an escalation in the defensive use of splitting and projection as she and Marcus tried to find ways of coping with the cruelty and pain that passed between them, and which over time constituted the sadomasochistic fit.

Hyatt-Williams (1998) suggests that enactments of aggression, violence, and murderousness are induced by psychic toxicity resulting from certain emotional experiences being unprocessed as a result of a lack of containment. Yakeley (2010) also suggests that if the child has internalised a pathological attachment relationship, then his or her capacity to regulate feelings is much reduced, and the individual is therefore more likely to express emotions in a primitive way, by violence towards self or others. Underscoring this point, Fonagy and Target (1995) also assert that violence is the product of the person's lack of a capacity for reflection or the ability to mentalise.

Taken together, this thinking seems to encapsulate the key elements that operated in the problematic and, at times, dangerous dynamic between Rhona and Marcus. However, by joining forces, Marcus and Rhona defeated our efforts to keep them apart, and because of this we were now experienced as the persecutory object and therefore we had to be killed off. Not surprisingly, Marcus and Rhona refused any further input from our service, and for a time things were quiet.

However, eight weeks later, Rhona was again the victim of Marcus' violence and was again desperate for our help. Marcus was interviewed by my colleague and stuck to his belief that Rhona had brought the violence on herself and that he would do it again if she didn't change her tune. In every other respect, Marcus was doing well; he had returned to school and there was even talk of him having a new girlfriend. Yet, Marcus had broken Rhona's nose in a fight, and she could see that, unless he got help, she was in danger of further attacks from him. In the joint meeting with her and Marcus, my colleague and I tried to broach the unwelcome subject of Marcus' recurring violence in the context of the disturbed mother–son relationship. Despite our efforts to directly address the emerging sadistic traits within Marcus' relationship with his mother and the very real possibility of him ending up in the youth justice system, Marcus refused to accept our recommendation that he be assessed by the local forensic services. The thinking behind this suggestion was that Marcus required a more specialised assessment that would help target an intervention to assist Marcus develop more control over his murderous rage and to better understand the pleasure he seemed to derive from hurting others. Although Rhona was in agreement with this suggestion, Marcus would not give his consent and made it very clear that he would not attend any appointments offered by the forensic services. Additionally, Rhona's reluctance to press charges against her son, her willingness to continue living with him, and the fact that Marcus was not sectionable under the Mental Health Act rendered us helpless in effecting change. Despite offering further meetings, Rhona and Marcus went to ground, and the last we heard was that Marcus had moved into his girlfriend's family home and Rhona herself was in a relationship with a new partner.

Conclusion

In this chapter, I have attempted to describe the emergence of a sado-masochistic relationship between a mother and her fourteen-year-old son. The intergenerational failure in containment and the prevailing attachment issues created the specific conditions under which sadism emerged. The son's struggle to contain his own wish for revenge on a mother who failed to atone for her abuse led to a particular dynamic that resulted in a dangerous dance concerning closeness and distance. The strategies both partners applied to manage their situation only served to intensify the battle between them. Despite our efforts to work with the dynamic, we found ourselves in a sadomasochistic alliance with mother and son, as they joined forces against us and effectively defeated our efforts to break the toxic link. Nevertheless, it seems possible that our presence and thinking did help to some extent in allowing a separation to occur and for the abuse to stop. Furthermore, the fact that mother and son were both able to forge new relationships indicates a possibility towards developmental strivings. On the other hand, it is also possible that the unresolved sadomasochistic fit finds yet another lock in future relationships, begging the question as to the direction and effectiveness of treatment interventions in this particular family constellation.

References

Barnow, S., Spitzer, C., Grabe, H. J., Kessler, C., & Freyberger H. J. (2006). Individual characteristics, familial experience, and psychopathology in children of mothers with borderline personality disorder. *Journal of the American Academy of Child and Adolscent Psychiatry, 45*: 965–972.

Bateman, A. W. (1998). Thick- and thin-skinned organisations and enactment in borderline and narcissistic disorder. *International Journal of Psychoanalysis, 79*: 13–25.

Fonagy, P., & Target, M. (1995). Understanding the violent patient: the use of the body and the role of the father. *International Journal of Psychoanalysis, 76*: 487–501.

Freud, S. (1905d). *Three Essays on the Theory of Sexuality. The Standard Edition of the Complete Psychological Works of Sigmund Freud, 7*. London: Hogarth.

Freud, S. (1914c). On narcissism: an introduction. *The Standard Edition of the Complete Psychological Works of Sigmund Freud, 14*: 67–102. London: Hogarth.

Glasser, M. (1996). Aggression and sadism in the perversions. In: I. Rosen (Ed.), *Sexual Deviation* (3rd edn, pp. 279–299). New York: Oxford University.

Hyatt-Williams, A. (1998). *Cruelty, Violence and Murder: Understanding the Criminal Mind*. New Jersey: Northvale.

Krafft-Ebing, R. (1898). *Psychopathia Sexualis: A Medico-Legal Study* (Trans.). Oxford: F. A. Davis.

Motz, A. (2014). *Toxic Couples: The Psychology of Domestic Violence*. London: Routledge/Taylor and Francis.

Myers, W. C., Burket, R. C., & Husted, D. S. (2006). Sadistic personality disorder and co-morbid mental illness in adolescent psychiatric inpatients. *Journal of American Academic Psychiatry and the Law, 34*: 61–71.

NICE (2013). Antisocial behavior and conduct disorders in children and young people: recognition and management. http://www.nice.org.uk/guidance/cg158

Rutter, M. (1985). Resilience in the face of adversity: protective factors and resistance to psychiatric factors. *British Journal of Psychiatry, 147*: 598–611.

Salekin, R. T., & Frick, P. J. (2005). Psychotherapy in children and adolescents: the need for a developmental perspective. *Journal of Abnormal Child Psychology, 33*: 403–409.

Steiner, J. (1993). *Psychic Retreats: Pathological Organisations in Psychotic, Neurotic and Boderline Patients*. London: Routledge.

Welldon, E. (2012). Couples who kill: the malignant bonding. In: J. Adlam, A. Aiyegbusi, P. Kleinot, A. Motz, & C. Scanlon (Eds.), *The Therapeutic Milieu under Fire: Security and Insecurity in Forensic Mental Health* (pp. 162–174). London: Jessica Kingsley.

World Health Organization (2005). *International Classification of Diseases and Related Health Problems*, Tenth Revision.

Yakeley, J. (2010). *Working with Violence: A Contemporary Psychoanalytic Approach*. Basingstoke: Palgrave Macmillan.

CHAPTER THREE

Working with sadism: an embodied relational approach

Morit Heitzler

Introduction

In this chapter, I present my work as an embodied-relational therapist with a young woman who, in her adolescence, was a victim of a gang of paedophiles. At the time of the abuse, my client, Molly, was one of several teenage girls who were systematically groomed by a ring of men who used the girls as prostitutes. These men formed part of a network of paedophiles who subjugated and forcibly subjected the teenage girls to sadistic sexual perversions, inflicting terror, pain, and suffering upon them during a developmentally crucial phase in their sexual maturation. In this chapter, I describe the therapeutic process and the possibilities as well as challenges of working with this client from an embodied-relational perspective. The emergent themes of sadism and sexual perversion are discussed within their wider theoretical context.

Molly came to see me seven months after a court trial in which she had testified against her attackers. She had attended the court trial alone, far from home, and heavily pregnant with her second child. For two weeks, she was challenged and cross-examined as she repeatedly told her story in the presence of most of the abusers (all of whom she recognised). This intense experience re-triggered the trauma that Molly

41

had so far been able to push away into a dark corner of her psyche, and it was this that impelled her to seek therapeutic help.

Having had a variety of unsatisfying previous treatments, Molly pursued a determined referral route to seek me out as a trauma specialist who integrates a wide range of therapeutic approaches, including specifically body-oriented, "somatic" trauma therapy.

I have written elsewhere (Heitzler, 2008) about my way of integrating different approaches to trauma work within an underlying relational framework.

There is increasing evidence from affective and trauma-based neuroscience that the "talking therapies", whilst accessing the cognitive residue and narrative memory of the event, have limited effect in processing the biological and neurological roots of trauma. This is because cognitive processing and mental reflection are disabled and go "offline" during the threatening experience itself. This also happens during flashbacks and when memories get triggered later on. Thus, somatic trauma therapies have come to the fore as treatments of choice for trauma. Somatic trauma therapy (Rothschild, 2000), somatic experiencing (Levine, 1997), and the sensori-motor approach (Ogden, 2006), whilst having slightly different models and methodologies, all provide tools for holistic processing of post-traumatic stress trapped on all body–mind levels in the client's system. This is an area for which eye movement desensitisation and reprocessing (EMDR) therapy has also been shown to be effective.

Molly had endured and survived the horrific ordeal she was put through. Now an adult, she lived with her partner and was bringing up their two children. Whilst outwardly she appeared to be functioning in an almost normal way, all kinds of apparently innocuous everyday tasks and events were triggering subliminal trauma symptoms. Molly had correctly identified she needed an embodied practitioner to recognise the subtle bodily manifestations of her post-traumatic stress disorder (PTSD), this round-the-clock re-traumatisation process behind her otherwise convincing coping strategies and façade. She needed an integrative and embodied trauma therapy in order to get beyond her previously habitual "barely coping" state of chronic PTSD and often robotic and de-personalised "plain survival" towards engaging in life.

Molly's therapy with me was ongoing at the time of writing this chapter. Whilst I have Molly's consent to discuss her therapy, I have taken care to conceal the identities of people mentioned here.

Brief history

Molly grew up on a council estate in a small town in the north of England. She was the elder of two daughters born to an alcoholic mother and a father whom she described as being absent, cut off, warm at times but prone to lose his temper at any moment. As a child, Molly remembers screaming hysterically when witnessing her parents' frequent violent and abusive brawls. Aged eight, Molly became the sole carer for her newly born sister. She recalled that it felt safer to push her pram through dark streets than remain in the house where her parents were throwing chairs and swearing at each other. Molly excelled at school, as studying provided her with an escape from her troubled home life, where her baby sister was constantly crying and her mother had withdrawn into post-natal depression. Molly's high academic achievements made her unpopular with her classmates, and although they did not dare to openly bully her, as she was tough and knew how to fight back, they would often mock her for being clever.

As she grew older, Molly began to skip school, preferring the company of other teenagers who hung out in the city-centre coffee shops. It was here that she was first approached by some older, charming men. She felt drawn to one in particular, a handsome man named Hamdi who had shiny dark eyes and who looked at her in a way that made her feel special, wanted. Soon, he became her hero, the object of her love and of her dreams. Hamdi and his friends often invited her to meet in town, bought her drinks and sweets, and would sit for hours listening to her, telling her their stories, bringing her small presents, and sharing with her exciting accounts of their young adult lives. Molly fell head over heels in love with Hamdi. She felt understood and cared for by him in a way that she had not previously experienced. She believed he was going to compensate for all the neglect, emotional deprivation, and abuse she had experienced at home. He was different from her father and all the other men at the estate, and he wanted her. For the first time in her life, Molly felt what she had always longed for: to feel loved, wanted, and appreciated.

With time, more of Hamdi's friends joined them when they met, but she was always the only girl, which she liked, as it made her feel special. They invited her to parties when they would all sit together in a room somewhere, drinking, smoking marijuana, listening to music, chatting, and laughing. Often, they would talk in their mother tongue, which Molly did not understand, but she would not mind—she would curl up in Hamdi's arms and doze off, lulled by the familiar sound of their voices.

Then, slowly, things changed. The sense of warmth and security was replaced by new and scary experiences: sex, violence, and heavier drugs. When she was twelve years old, they forced the first heroin injection into her, and then the second. Soon they did not have to force any more, she asked for it, and they always gave it to her, although they did not take it themselves. She was asked to "be nice" to their friends, people she did not know but who wanted to do weird sexual things to her. Often, what they did hurt her. Then she was not asked any more, and the men were not called "friends" but "customers". They travelled from far away, had different accents, and they all hurt her. She did not mind much, as long as the men kept giving her heroin and marijuana and talked to her as if they were all still friends, as long as Hamdi reassured her with his soft voice and warm eyes, that she was still special and beautiful to him. Molly lost weight, she had needle marks on her arms, her pale skin grew yellow, and she was totally addicted to heroin. She would be out late at night, looking for drugs, and also looking for the men who provided her with heroin, especially when they did not come to meet her.

At some point, in the midst of the drug-induced fog that her life had turned into, social services got involved following the request of her mother, who could not cope with her daughter's behaviour any more. Molly was moved into care. Now, the men would wait for her outside the care home, taking her to anonymous, empty rooms with dirty, graffiti-covered walls. She often wondered, upon waking up from another unconscious stupor, whether the blood on the dirty walls was hers. She would look at her battered body, at the yellow-purple marks on her arms, thighs, neck, belly, and wonder what had been done to her. Her body ached all over. Sometimes she would escape by breaking a window, running with bare feet in wintry frozen streets to the police station, where nobody believed her stories. The police would keep her for the night and then would deliver her back to the care home, where her social worker disbelieved her, saying that Molly was inventing stories as an excuse for her "poor life choices". When Molly insisted that her stories were true, and gave the names of her abusers, her social worker felt Molly was hallucinating, and Molly was prescribed anti-psychotic drugs instead.

So Molly ran away again, looking for heroin, looking for "them" in the hope that life would revert to how it had been at the beginning: before she was hit and made to "entertain customers", to a time when Hamdi would make her feel special and loved as they sat with his friends smoking marijuana, listening to music, and laughing together, just like before.

During the first few weeks of my work with Molly, as her story unfolded in my consulting room, I was moved by her courage and impressed by her profound intelligence and strength. I was struck by her ability to love her partner and their children and engage with life in a surprisingly healthy way. However, as the therapeutic relationship developed, she was able to let me know that her nights were haunted by nightmares, that she barely slept. Intimacy was difficult, and she found it hard to trust any man. She suffered frequent panic attacks. Her body was chronically tense and her breathing restricted. All these symptoms had worsened after her appearance in court. I accepted and embraced her vulnerability, helped her make sense of it, and invited its expression, and Molly learned, maybe for the first time in her life, to embrace the scared screaming toddler within her as well as the horrified, tortured young adolescent. Our work together was at times challenging, walking a fine line between processing the traumas she had endured and making sure she would not be re-traumatised by us remembering them together, but during that period I was not yet being pushed beyond my comfort zone—not until the particular session when Molly was ready to share with me one of her most disturbing memories.

A night of horror

Two years into child prostitution, Molly decided she did not want to serve one particular customer who hurt her more than others did. So she said she was menstruating, as this often put off some customers who liked to cause her to bleed instead. However, Hamdi's brother did not believe her. He shoved his hand into her underwear and showed the others standing by that she was lying. Then he bit her, as he often did when he was angry, but that evening he bit her really hard. With help from some of the other men (not the customers, but Hamdi and his friends), he threw her into the boot of their car and drove off. They drove for some time.

When the car stopped, a very frightened Molly was dragged out. It was dark and cold; she could smell the freshness of the rain in the forest, and she guessed that they were in the woods, just outside town. Hamdi's brother kicked her and forced her to kneel down. He sent one of the guys to bring the big machete they always kept at the back of the car. "You white pig", he was screaming: "You lied to us, you white pig, now you will get what pigs deserve." He grabbed her hair, pulling tight, yanking her head back, and putting the machete to her neck. "I will slaughter you, you stinking pig!" Molly was crying. Kneeling on the ground, she begged "Please, please, don't kill me, please, I'll do whatever you say, please don't kill me!" But he kept shouting and kicking her, getting angrier and louder with every curse and blow. Then he called his brother and commanded him to take his trousers off. Holding the machete to Molly's neck, still pulling her hair, he ordered Molly to give Hamdi oral sex. They all stood around and watched, drinking whiskey. Nobody spoke, they were all afraid of Hamdi's brother, especially when he lost his temper. When Hamdi was done, another man was told to take off his pants. The machete hurt her neck as Hamdi's brother dug it a bit deeper into her flesh, she could feel the blood trickling down her throat. "You do him now and then I'll kill you, you white stinking pig." Molly "did" him, and then the next one, and the next. At some point, she was sick, she did not know any more what her body was doing. She could hear them phoning their friends, then more cars arrived with men she did not know. One by one, they took their trousers off and came to her. They were not silent any more; they were laughing and encouraging each other. The lights of the cars formed a circle; the trees grew high and dark around them. She was kneeling for what seemed like hours, more and more men kept arriving, and all the time the machete at her throat, the hand pulling at her hair, and curses ringing in her ears. Through the numbness and the fog, she heard an unfamiliar voice saying: "Let's stop this, this is sick", but they did not stop. At some point, she lost consciousness. Hamdi's brother woke her up with a kick, yanking her head hard. He laughed, and poured his whiskey on her, poking her belly with his machete.

Then, all of a sudden, it all stopped. They went into their cars and drove away, leaving Molly lying alone on the cold ground. It was very quiet and pitch black. Molly was scared. She managed to pull herself up and stood there swaying. She did not know where to go, but somehow she remembered that she had her mobile phone with her and it had a flashlight. She turned that light on and ran; falling down and getting back up, she continued running. Not knowing where she was going, not able to think, she ran for a long time until, as if by a miracle, she found herself outside the woods, on the outskirts of the city. She was frozen, and her body was covered with blood, vomit, and semen. She had no idea where she could go, looking like that. She needed her fix, the hunger for the drug was getting stronger. She could not think. So she called them. And they came and picked her up, chatting to her on the way back, as if nothing had happened. They took her to one of the rooms they used and she had a bath, and a stiff drink, and the drug. They were there, too, just those she knew, the familiar faces. Hamdi's brother was not there, though, and they all looked more relaxed and happy in his absence. It was all so normal, so easy-going, that she felt sort of OK. "I have done something bad", she told herself "I lied and refused, and I was punished for it, that was all".

After that, things carried on as usual—the event was forgotten. Only at night, if the heroin was not strong enough, Molly could still feel the machete cutting through her skin. Her dreams were filled with decapitated bodies, and she would get sick whenever she smelled the scent of trees after the rain.

Working with my countertransference

Molly had been my last client for that day and when I closed the door to my consulting room behind me, I could not bring myself to enter my home right away, as I usually do. I restlessly walked around in the yard, breathing deeply, trying in vain to ground myself back in my body. After some time, I went in and busied myself with cooking dinner, mechanically going through the motions. At the dinner table with my husband, I was unable to eat. I felt alienated from him, unable to engage in his conversation, and disconnected from myself, almost de-personalised. The next few days passed in a surreal haze as images from Molly's story flooded my mind. A deadening numbness engulfed me between these flashbacks. During this time and for a few weeks afterwards, for personal reasons, my supervisor was unavailable. I felt unable to share this traumatising story with any of my peers. I felt alone with what I had heard, and what I was experiencing, viscerally, in my own body. Like Molly, I was alone with the after-shock.

Looking at my countertransference response, I was exploring the possibility of over-identification with the victim. Was I being too open to absorbing the trauma, was I over-identified with my client, losing my therapeutic boundaries and position to the point of becoming incapacitated and useless to her as a therapist? Or was I being present and available for "interactive regulation" (Schore, 1999), allowing myself to be affected in a way that was necessary for continuing therapeutic engagement and eventual healing?

It is important to remember that, whilst being in principle capable of narratively remembering the trauma in the safety of our co-created space, in all the intervening years Molly never actually had entertained these memories in any sustained fashion. They had only manifested as incoherent flashbacks and nightmares. In contrast, we had systematically prepared the encounter with that night over many weeks, with me carefully "titrating" her exposure to it step by step, attuned to her autonomic nervous system responses and using EMDR to process the build-up towards it.

During the session described above, I believe that it was my ability to stay present in the moment with whatever Molly shared that allowed her to be present herself whilst re-counting what had previously been unbearable. It was my embodied presence in the room that enabled her to stay embodied herself. But receiving it on an embodied level was only the first stage of my work as her therapist. In order to model processing rather than dissociating the trauma, I now had to stick with it: to visualise and digest it, and think about it. It is the therapist's capacity to contain and integrate those previously dissociated aspects of the trauma that creates the safe container: as I am able to regulate the emotional and energetic impact of the trauma on my own embodied system, I can provide the regulation needed by the client and thus the foundation for the work to carry on.

This was my rationale for processing the session in the way I will describe now, and why I insisted on feeling the horror of it in my own body. In the following week, my first reactions—flashbacks and active numbness—were replaced by a strong pull towards avoiding the whole thing: the temptation to dissociate was immense. But I knew I had to overcome the fear to fully take that horror in and to do what Molly did when she came to see me: to stop running away. So I sat in a closed room, called upon all my resources to support me, and took myself, using images and visualisation, back to that wood. In my fantasy, I stood there, unseen, and looked at it all, looked at it happening. I stayed with it as much as I could, seeing, hearing, smelling, sensing. When I could not bear it any longer, I stopped and cried and shook, and felt the waves of nausea and paralysing fear. Then I took a deep breath and went back again. For a long time, I did that: bore witness to that horrific ritualistic abuse of power, of domination and humiliation, of sexual exploitation and rage, of plain fear of dying. I was there; I felt it in my body. I lived it not as if it were happening to me, but as a present witness who is not averting her gaze.

My main temptation, apart from looking away, was to take over, to chase all the abusers away and take Molly by the hand, lead her away to a safe, warm place, where I could hold her and look after her. I noticed that impulse inside me—the impulse to be the rescuer, the saviour, the idealised protective mother. I understood that Molly was longing for me to provide this all the time, but I also understood that this was not what she really needed from me. For us to be able to truly process the trauma, rather than being possessed by it, she needed me to NOT dissociate. So I stayed with things as they really happened and watched that "movie" to the bitter chilling end. I did that a few times, until I could look at it from the beginning through to the end without having to stop. This was important, as it is recognised in trauma work and EMDR that the capacity to remember the whole narrative of a trauma without becoming overwhelmed constitutes one of the criteria of it having been sufficiently processed to not interfere with everyday life any more.

I then went out into the fields surrounding my home, to the vast open space of Nature, offering me comfort and recuperation. I was exhausted and drained, but I felt hopeful. I thought about Molly and about the stories she often shared with me of her children. I thought about her deep love for them and how joyful and proud she was of them. I thought about her warmth and her intelligence, her courage and generosity, her common sense and ability to understand and accept imperfections, and I knew that we would win this battle; I knew that Molly could heal.

The key therapeutic factor: an embodied relational presence

It has been a growing recognition throughout the psychotherapeutic field that bodies—the client's and the therapist's—have traditionally been excluded from the therapeutic process. Nowhere is this more established now than in trauma work, where the significance of bodily experience has become firmly recognised (Levine, 1997), generating the modern range of somatic trauma therapies (Ogden, 2006; Rothschild, 2000). Because during trauma those parts of the brain involved in thinking and in processing emotions (the cerebral cortex and some limbic structures) shut down, trauma is experienced first and foremost in the body; it is in the body that trauma is stored and remembered (van der Kolk, 1996); and it is in the body that it *needs* to be healed and that it *is experienced* as healed—that is the crucial criterion that matters to most trauma survivors: whether the trauma is no longer experienced in the body. Having experienced the trauma as an unexploded bomb of somatic reactions, which they feel at the mercy of, as it is liable to be uncontrollably and overwhelmingly triggered at any moment, the trauma survivor has a profound and recognisable "felt sense" when that bomb is no longer there, no longer permanently threatening from within.

What is less clearly appreciated in the somatic approaches to trauma is the involvement of the therapist's body—the intersubjective and relational dimension. It is understood that the therapist's empathic engagement can lead to "compassion fatigue" and "vicarious traumatisation" (Rothschild, 2006) through a process of absorbing the clients' trauma conceptualised as occurring via the brain's mirror neurons. This raises the question of how the therapist can be protected against the dangers of secondary traumatisation, when on the other hand it is also understood that it is via "interactive regulation" (Schore, 2001) by the therapist that the client's traumatically incapacitated "auto-regulation" of hyper-arousal is increasingly restored.

How can we reconcile these contradictory requirements, and what actually *is* the therapist's internal process in the face of shocking and terrifying experiences brought into the consulting room by the client?

Therapists tend to "cope" with this dilemma by resorting to one of two fixed positions: a guiding, directive, quasi-medical "doctor" stance, or a reassuring protective "mother-healer" role. Both positions fit with the kind of distancing reaction to trauma that victims come to anticipate as socially "normal": they expect the mind of the other to dissociate, registering at best the meanings of the words and the story they tell, but to remain removed from the unbearable feelings and sensations. A client expects no different when first coming to a therapist.

There is strong evidence that the client is subliminally well aware of the therapist's relational stance and presence, and that this significantly influences the working alliance and the outcome of therapy. Schore (1994) postulates right-brain-to-right-brain communication as the foundation of the therapeutic endeavour, constituting the neurological basis for what Lyons-Ruth (1999) calls "implicit relational knowing". Infant research has lent credibility to the body-based bonding of "primary intersubjectivity" (Beebe & Lachmann, 2013; Trevarthen, 1979, p. 321) which involves pre-reflexive dyadic interactions. Such empathic capacities acquired in infancy remain crucial elements of emotional communication throughout the life span and are thus highly relevant for the therapeutic encounter. The therapist's body—and its spontaneous reaction—constitutes the ground of safety, just as the mother's body does for the infant.

Therefore a crucial question is: how is the therapist's presence experienced *by the client* during the narrating and processing of such memories? The client cannot help but unconsciously scan to determine where the therapist is situated along the spectrum between being empathically connected or clinically distant. There is a profound and developmentally deeply rooted purpose to such scanning on the client's part: they are trying to get an instinctive sense of how available this supposedly helpful person is to interactively regulate their pain. How overwhelmed and blindly reactive against the pain is *their* body?

Having evolved as a therapist in a community of practitioners that has developed body psychotherapy in the United Kingdom over the last twenty years, I take embodied attunement for granted as the foundation of my therapeutic presence in any context. Body psychotherapy has long recognised the interweaving of physical, emotional, and mental processes in all human experience, and has accumulated decades of therapeutic practice focusing on the client's body–mind rather than predominantly verbal interaction. So, "implicit relational knowing" constitutes my "baseline", rooted in the assumption that my "embodied countertransference" (Soth, 2005) informs me about my client's inner world, including unconscious and dissociated experiences.

However, in relation to Molly, an embodied-relational perspective took me way beyond the usual comfort zone of my therapeutic position: her pain and humiliation during her sadistic torture, her fear of being slaughtered at any point, were visceral experiences that went straight inside me. My solidly established embodied attunement with Molly meant that her night of horrors registered directly in my own body–mind system: I felt it in my tightly constricting belly, in my sunken heart, in my heavy, numb legs, the sense of nausea in my throat, the paralysing fear, and the compelling impulse to dissociate. This direct transmission of the victim experience and its impact on me would have been totally overwhelming, if not for the years of working with trauma, which had taught me to use my body not just as a means of receiving this kind of communication, but also as a resource in processing it. During the session, I used some breathing and grounding techniques that enabled me to stay present and engaged with Molly, and only after the session had I surrendered to the urgent need to dissociate.

Theoretical conceptualisation of sadism

According to the Diagnostic and Statistical Manual of Mental Disorders (DSM-III, 1980), sadistic personality disorder (removed in later versions of the DSM) is marked by the use of physical violence or cruelty to establish dominance in a relationship. The sadistic person hurts and demeans other people around them, often in public, deriving pleasure from inflicting such humiliation; they will also demonstrate amusement or pleasure at the suffering of others, both people and animals.

To summarise the psychodynamic literature, we find the assumption that sadism results from deep-seated feelings of inferiority, or from the person being themselves severely abused or demeaned as a child. Sinason (2014) suggests that many people who were abused during childhood tend to project their helplessness, fear, and rage onto the victim and, in doing so, attempt to disown and overcome the vulnerable child-part within themselves. Celenza writes:

> sadomasochistic scenarios can be conceived as attempts to omnipotently control overwhelming experience. Sexuality overwhelms by definition, requiring, as it does, tolerance of dependency, vulnerability, and self-revelation. Ultimately, orgasm requires moments of unconsciousness, a highly threatening experience for those with deep mistrust. Early experience will inevitably be evoked during sexual experience.
>
> (Celenza, 2014, p. 113)

Thus, she argues, the sadist tries to conquer these early vulnerabilities by taking a power-over position, aiming to achieve ultimate control precisely to counteract these challenges inherent in sexual acts. This thought is echoed by Benjamin, who states, "domination begins with the attempt to deny dependency" (1988, p. 52). Messler-Davies suggests that children who were sexually traumatised over time, especially by a parent, "will internalize and identify with those aspects of the perpetrator, who is also a loved and trusted figure in the child's life. Thus, children become identified with the aggressor as through this identification, the child attempts to preserve her bond to the perpetrator by becoming like him" (Messler-Davies, 1994, p. 171).

De-humanisation beyond objectification

Setting Molly's abuse within a theoretical context, it becomes possible to consider the abusers' own personal histories that might have led them to act out their wounds through ritualised sexually perverted sadistic attacks on a young, defenceless child. I have come to group the abusers into three categories: the main perpetrator, Hamdi's brother; the victim-perpetrators, Hamdi and his other "friends" who had established relationships with Molly for about two years; and the other men, strangers and "customers" who were "invited to the party".

Hamdi's brother became infuriated at Molly's refusal to surrender to his commands—in an attempt to re-instate his control, he submitted her to prolonged physical, sexual, and emotional torture. His main degrading comment, "white pig", referring to the most disgusting, hated, and degraded animal in the Muslim tradition, indicated this man's rage with British society, and his place as a non-white person in that society. I know from Molly's stories that this group of young men often faced racist comments and that Hamdi's brother did not have any financially secure or socially respected position. I imagine that his accumulated rage—the result of years of racial discrimination, ongoing humiliation, and powerlessness—found an outlet in his attack on Molly, and was his way of taking revenge for feeling degraded himself. In his racist comments towards her, he evoked similar feelings in the second group, those young men who knew Molly and perhaps would not be inclined themselves to take such severe measures in "punishing" her. His comment united them against her and what she symbolised at that moment: she was no longer the person they knew, she was a "white" woman, whom they could humiliate as revenge for all the humiliation they had had to endure. When she was the "white pig", they were no longer the "Pakis" (a derogatory term for people of Pakistani origin).

At the Centre of Research and Education in Forensic Psychology, University of Kent, Alleyne et al. (2014) found that violent behaviour in youth gangs relies on "moral disengagement strategies", disconnecting them from the acts they commit by dehumanising their victims. Lammers states, "dehumanization [is] the process of denying essential elements of 'humanness' in other people and perceiving them as objects or animals" (Lammers, 2011, p. 113).

Throughout, Molly had been objectified by her abusers; however, during that torturous night in the woods, this escalated into Hamdi's brother dehumanising Molly by calling her "white pig", enabling himself and the other men to morally disengage from her. In reducing Molly to the "white pig", the prior established relationship between her and the perpetrators had been obliterated: she had become the receptacle into which racial, non-personal hate was being evacuated. This was my own best approximation in response to Molly's questions searching for meaning: "Why did they do it to me? How could they have done that?"

The experience of the abuser in the countertransference

These kinds of questions are pervasive amongst survivors of abuse, both for valid philosophical and for dangerously self-blaming and self-shaming reasons. Psychodynamic therapists are familiar with the uncanny experience that their countertransference gives them disturbing access to some of the "answers" which shed light on the abusive dynamic: in my work with trauma survivors, I often have the spontaneous, unpleasant experience of embodying the abuser in my thoughts, impulses, feelings, and fantasies. Such embodied countertransference reactions (Messler-Davies, 1994, p. 151) allow the therapist to gain first-hand experience and a "felt sense" of all the poles of the "triangle of abuse" (Heitzler, 2011, p. 19), historically, in the transference, and also as the presence of the abuser as an "internal object" in the client's system (Heitzler, 2011, p. 23).

It is often tempting for us as therapists to polarise against the sadist and keep our own sense of self intact by taking the moral high ground. Behind our shock and disgust in the face of cold-hearted cruelty, we might detect our own fear of being the next prey or, indeed, of discovering traces of the perpetrator in ourselves. Either position may be experienced as threatening to our self-image and sense of integrity—it is understandable, although counterproductive, that many therapists shy away from conscious identification with the abuser. To engage with *all* split-off, dissociated parts of the trauma, and function as the "regulating other" who holds the full impact of the trauma whilst the client is working at her own pace towards integration (Heitzler, 2011, p. 24), the therapist's ability to inhabit the perpetrator as a felt body–mind experience is paramount.

Being thus used to monitoring my embodied countertransference, I was surprised to notice that in my work with Molly I did not have the experience of embodying the abusers. I had various reactions *towards* the perpetrators, during and after the sessions, such as rage, fear, disgust, hate; and I noticed that these were somatic and affective reactions that came either from my identification with Molly or from the witness position. Because a felt sense of the abusers, their impulses, or reality just did not arise in my own body–mind, I wondered whether I had unconsciously chosen to identify with the victim and exempted myself from the unsavoury task of identifying with the perpetrators.

Whenever Molly was angry, she felt betrayed and brutalised and wanted her abusers punished by imprisonment, but she never conveyed any need for stronger forms of revenge. She was not enraged. She wanted to understand why and how this could have happened, and for the perpetrators to acknowledge the injustice and cruelty of what they had done. "How is it possible that this is all she needs?" I was often left wondering. As the work continued, I realised that the only manifestations of Molly's rage were towards her alcoholic mother's emotional neglect and deprivation, not towards her abusers—somehow she had not internalised them. Hamdi and his friends appeared to represent an idealised maternal figure to whom she had once attached and upon whom she had depended. Despite dropping their seductive masks and becoming abusive and life-threatening, Molly held on to those shreds of warmth and positive affirmation, hoping to re-instate what she perceived as the loving relationship they once had offered and promised—this (and her heroin dependency) may explain what led her to telephoning them after emerging from the woods. This continuing primal hope constitutes a straightforward re-enactment of her early relationship with her mother: to this day, Molly imagines that her mother will one day come back to her senses and recover her proper mothering functions. As the perpetrators had not been internalised, I could not get an embodied sense of "them" in the countertransference, I could only feel them as "others", as she did.

Working with the sadist or internalised perpetrator

So far I have focused mainly on the victim position, as described by Molly during her therapy with me, rather than the perpetrator of sadism. Molly's identification with the perpetrator was not as deeply rooted in her primal feelings as I have seen in other cases, where sadistic abuse carries echoes of developmentally earlier, incestuous acts of sadism and cruelty which have then become introjected as internal abuser figures. However, in the later stages of her process, as Molly got more in touch with her rage towards her mother, we did need to work with her internalised perpetrator, diluted as it was. I will therefore end this chapter by touching briefly on the relational dynamic and the therapeutic position required when engaging with the sadist rather than with the victim of sadism.

One of the theories I found most useful in working with perpetrators is Jessica Benjamin's (2004) notion of the doer–done-to complementarity: often, the perpetrator has their own experience of being on the receiving end of sadism, and when this experience gets triggered, the perpetrator is liable to enact it externally towards their victim. What breaks this torturous chain is if the doer–done-to complementarity— rooted in primitive states where the other is experienced only as an object or a part-object, not a person—can be transcended by humanising the rage in the contact with the therapist, thus establishing a third, reflective, containing position.

The sadist is stuck in a continuous negative feedback loop, driven to constantly exacerbate a battle between the polarities of an internalised object relation which he cannot escape, generating an interlocking state of hyper-arousal fuelled both by fear and rage. The therapeutic task is, therefore, to humanise and interpersonally regulate that feedback loop and open it up. As in trauma work, this requires that the therapist be experienced as involved and implicated in the battle, by "inserting" herself in it, by entering the enactment, rather than remaining a clinical observer. Through that engagement and lack of avoidance, which the sadist has come to expect from people who are naturally frightened of him, the therapist can gain some regulatory influence over this cyclic dynamic, which stops it from remaining an exclusively internal, self-perpetuating loop. The sadist's life story has taught him that his rage cannot ever be contained, because every time it gets expressed, it appears to destroy the relationship one way or the other. So the main question for the therapist is: how can I sufficiently participate in the

enactment, so the rage can be *met* this time, rather than once again having a destructive impact on the contact?

As a body-oriented therapist, working in a tradition that has often
idealised and over-emphasised the catharsis of raw emotion, I view the
"rage system" (Panksepp, 2004)[1] as a biologically rooted evolutionary
process that is not easily contained by the cortex. When rage cannot
be auto-regulated internally, it is through the expression of rage being
met by an embodied "other" that interpersonal containment may occur.
This mainly embodied, non-verbal experience depends on therapists
regulating their own fear internally in such a way that they neither
retaliate with threats nor withdraw, thus communicating a refusal to be
dominated by either fear or rage. This, hopefully, will allow a different
experience to emerge, breaking the repetitive feedback loop previously
experienced by the patient, and mobilising the brain's capacity for neu-
roplasticity, creating new neurological pathways, manifesting a more
containable experience when the rage is triggered again in the future.

Conclusion

Whether it is the need to control and dominate the external object of
longing, or the fear of the internal vulnerability, the sadist usually projects
his own victimised self onto the person he tortures: he feels compelled
to punish the internal "victim self", which he loathes, and rather than
experiencing it internally, he evacuates it into an "other" and enacts the
punishment externally, thus keeping his identification with the abuser
ongoing. Victimisation has many faces and expressions, including—as
suggested above—cultural components as possible triggers for feelings
of helplessness and inferiority, which can in turn unleash sadistic rage.
One of the main challenges in working with sadism therapeutically is
how to simultaneously hold both extreme polarities of feeling: the perpetrator's position alongside the victim's. This requires the therapist
to be in touch within herself with the depths of these raw emotions,
capable of embodying them, rather than constructing a cognitive and
verbal position that is habitually dissociated, as the client will suspect
such distancing and mistrust it.

Working with the victim or with the perpetrator alike, the therapist's willingness and ability to put herself on the line and engage fully
with the shadow aspects of her own personality is crucial. To be fully
available in this way is, of course, always our conscious intention, but

working with sadism can challenge our willingness in extreme ways, as it pushes us way beyond our comfort zone, into a dark abyss. However, this work is but another mirror, reflecting the distorted expressions of human suffering. As therapists, we are called upon to look into that scary mirror and, sometimes, be willing to see ourselves.

Note

1. Affective neuroscience has identified seven brain systems, each integrated in terms of anatomical, functional, and biochemical components and dedicated to a recognisable and distinct set of emotions. Each system has its evolutionary pathway that can be traced back to mammals and earlier species, allowing the assumption that each emotional sub-system must have had adaptive functions and purposes. Panksepp suggests: "The various positive affects indicate that animals are returning to 'comfort zones' that support survival, and negative affects reflect 'discomfort zones' that indicate that animals are in situations that may impair survival. They are ancestral tools for living—evolutionary memories of such importance that they were coded into the genome in rough form (as primary brain processes), which are refined by basic learning mechanisms (secondary processes) as well as by higher-order cognitions/thoughts (tertiary processes)" (Panksepp, 2010).

References

Alleyne, E., Fernandes, I., & Pritchard, E. (2014). Denying humanness to victims: how gang members justify violent behavior. *Group Processes and Intergroup Relations, 12*: 695–697.

American Psychiatric Association (1980). *Diagnostic and Statistical Manual of Mental Disorders*, Third Edition. Arlington, VA: American Psychiatric Publishing.

Bandura, A., Barbaranelli, C., Caprara, G. V., & Pastorelli, C. (1996). Mechanisms of moral dis-engagement in the exercise of moral agency. *Journal of Personality and Social Psychology, 71*: 364–374.

Beebe, B., & Lachmann, F. (2013). *The Origins of Attachment: Infant Research and Adult Treatment*. Hove, East Sussex: Routledge.

Benjamin, J. (1998). *Bonds of Love*. New York: Pantheon.

Benjamin, J. (2004). Beyond doer and done-to: an intersubjective view of thirdness. *Psychoanalytic Quarterly, 73*: 5–46.

Celenza, A. (2014). *Erotic Revelations: Clinical Applications and Perverse Scenarios*. London: Routledge.

Heitzler, M. (2009). Towards an integrative model of trauma therapy. In: L. Hartley (Ed.), *Contemporary Body Psychotherapy—The Chiron Approach* (pp. 177–193). Hove: Routledge.

Heitzler, M. (2011). Crowded intimacy—engaging multiple enactments in complex trauma work. *British Journal of Psychotherapy Integration, 8*: 15–26.

Heitzler, M. (2013). Broken boundaries, invaded territories: the challenges of containment in trauma work. *International Body Psychotherapy Journal, 12*: 28–41.

Lammers, J. (2011). Power increases dehumanization. *Group Processes and Intergroup Relations, 14*: 113–126.

Levine, P. (1997). *Waking the Tiger: Healing Trauma—The Innate Capacity to Transform Overwhelming Experiences*. Berkeley, CA: North Atlantic Books.

Messler-Davies, J., & Frawley, M. (1994). *Treating the Adult Survivor of Childhood Sexual Abuse: A Psychoanalytic Perspective*. New York: Basic Books.

Ogden, P., Minton, K., & Pain, C. (2006). *Trauma and the Body: A Sensorimotor Approach to Psychotherapy*. London: W. W. Norton.

Panksepp, J. (2004). *Affective Neuroscience: The Foundations of Human and Animal Emotions*. Oxford: Oxford University Press.

Panksepp, J. (2010). Affective neuroscience of the emotional brain mind: evolutionary perspectives and implications for understanding depression. *Dialogues in Clinical Neuroscience, 12*: 533–545.

Rothschild, B. (2000). *The Body Remembers*. London: W. W. Norton.

Rothschild, B. (2006). *Help for the Helper: The Psychophysiology of Compassion Fatigue and Vicarious Trauma*. London: W. W. Norton.

Schore, A. N. (1999). *Affect Regulation and the Origin of the Self*. London: Psychology Press.

Schore, A. N. (2001). The effects of early relational trauma on right brain development, affect regulation, and infant mental health. *Infant Mental Health Journal, 22*: 7–66.

Sinason, V. (2014). *Sexual Sadism in Ritual Abuse: The Dilemma of the Perpetrator*. Confer Seminar Series on Working Psychotherapeutically with Sadism, London.

Soth, M. (2005). Embodied countertransference. In: N. Totton (Ed.), *New Dimensions in Body Psychotherapy* (pp. 40–55). Maidenhead: Open University Press.

Trevarthen, C. (1979). Communication and cooperation in early infancy: a description of primary intersubjectivity. In: M. Bullowa (Ed.), *Before Speech: The Beginning of Interpersonal Communication* (pp. 321–347). London: Cambridge University Press.

Van der Kolk, B. A. (1996). Trauma and memory. In: B. A. van der Kolk, A. C. McFarlane, & L. Weisaeth (Eds.), *Traumatic Stress: The Effects of Overwhelming Experience on Mind, Body and Society* (pp. 279–302). New York, London: The Guilford Press.

CHAPTER FOUR

Sexual sadism in ritual abuse: the dilemma of the perpetrator

Valerie Sinason

Introduction

There is profound historical unfairness in the fact that acts of sadism gain their terminology from a man who was against capital punishment and torture at a time when such acts were common occurrences. The French aristocrat the Marquis de Sade (2 June 1740 to 2 December 1814) was a courageous politician, philosopher, and writer. During the French Revolution, he was elected delegate to the National Convention. His surname is used because of the pornographic work he wrote during his thirty-two years in prison with their unsurprising emphasis on violence, criminality, and attacks on the Catholic Church at a time when blasphemy was a serious crime. We could now consider that his encyclopaedic understanding of all perversion was both a defence against terror of dying and a way of containing within himself the brutal acts he witnessed (Glasser, 1996, 1998).

The Marquis de Sade had been imprisoned for assaulting a prostitute, for sex with a man, and for blasphemy. He had paid for the prostitute's services but was rougher than agreed. Such non-contracted roughness can make for difficult court cases in the twenty-first century in the West,

61

let alone in a period of publicly witnessed and condoned torture. Whilst his writing is imbued with sadism, it is not apparent that in actual life he was a sexual sadist, although he was clearly sexually disturbed. There is some information to suggest that he was first abused at the age of six by his uncle, an Abbe, and that could be part of the hatred he held for organised religion.

The term "sadism", as it is used now—the wish to be sexually aroused by torture and control—I will place into context as the focus of this chapter concerns sexual sadism in organised criminal groups, including those who use a religious or pseudo-religious context in order to generate greater fear.

Definitions

The work of Krafft-Ebing, an Austrian psychiatrist and author of the foundational *Psychopathia Sexualis* (1886), was crucial to any modern understanding of sexual sadism. He defined it as:

> The experience of sexual, pleasurable sensations (including orgasm) produced by acts of cruelty, bodily punishment afflicted on one's person or when witnessed in others, be they animals or human beings. It may also consist of an innate desire to humiliate, hurt, wound or even destroy others in order, thereby, to create sexual pleasure in oneself.
>
> (Krafft-Ebing, 1886, p. 109)

The understanding in this definition has remained consistent. The pain, distress, and humiliation of the victim is crucial to the sexual arousal and pleasure of the sadist. In other words, the sheer level of brutality and the physical effects caused to the victim are not the core of the definition; to be termed "sexual sadism", the impact on the victim is the issue rather than the level of brutality or the infliction of pain. For this reason, acts of necrophilia, however brutal to the body, do not necessarily come under a category of sexual sadism if the perpetrator believes the victim cannot feel it. Even an act of rape is not necessarily an act of sexual sadism.

Krafft-Ebing underlined the link between sexual arousal and murder (including cannibalism), necrophilia, specific injury to women both literal and symbolic, sadistic acts with animals, bestiality, sadism with other inanimate objects, and sadism that remains a fantasy. In cataloguing different signs of sexual disturbance, he drew attention to the treatment of adults as if they were animals, where, for instance, they were put into cages like dogs.

Sexual sadism is reportedly found predominately in males and is thought to begin usually in puberty. As our understanding of child abuse and abusing in children has improved, there is a growing awareness of earlier-onset sadistic behaviour; nevertheless, it becomes evident by early adulthood. Sexual sadism may begin with fantasies and, in some cases, these may never be acted upon or, alternatively, they might be acted out in milder forms of consensual sadomasochistic relationships. In non-consensual cases, the behaviour tragically continues and often escalates over time. The perpetrator experiences a need for increased violence in order to stimulate the sexual response. In other words, once a boundary has been crossed, which in itself can create excitement, the sexual response may become dulled or absent. This is why access to therapeutic treatment is so important. The further an adult enacts their sexual sadism, the harder it is to bear the emotional consequences of stopping. Additionally, by this stage, the criminal justice system is likely to have become involved, and to have stepped in, given the sexually sadistic ingredient in many serial murder cases as well as in explicitly sexual offences (Beeger et al., 1999). Hill et al. (2006) investigated which characteristics differentiated sexually sadistic from non-sadistic sexual murderers. Offenders with sexual sadism (36.7 per cent) were compared with offenders without this diagnosis (63.3 per cent). Besides the sexual sadistic symptoms, there were seven factors that discriminated best between the two groups: sexual masochism, sadistic personality disorder, isolation in childhood, multiple sexual homicide, previous rape, previous tendencies for similar behaviour, and long duration of the homicidal act.

Ever since we have had recorded history of warfare, there has been an understanding that whilst war involves killing, it does not have to involve sadism. Treatment of hostages was something to which the Romans devoted a great deal of ethical time. In a sketch on army recruiting, the British surreal comedy series Monty Python, broadcast by the BBC between 1969 and 1974, featured a would-be recruit who wanted to join the army to kill people whilst the recruiting officer spoke of all the qualifications and travel he could get by joining the army! We have always historically been aware of those who use legally or culturally santioned aggression to others in ways that are enhanced with something extra, something disturbed and perverse.

In cases of female sexual sadism, onset is considered to be later and is often triggered by relationships with men who want to be dominated. Tragically, as with Rosemary West, a British woman who collaborated with her husband in the torture and murder of ten young women between 1971 and 1987, we witness the way trauma-bonded abused females end up as co-conspirators in sexual sadism. We witness the way some abused females end up as co-conspirators in sexual sadism. Some women survive the initial trauma by bonding and identifying with their abusers to the extent of joining in with them.

Paradoxically, while sexual sadism appears more common in men, there seems to be a predominance of female dominatrixes in sado-masochistic pornography (Weinberg, 1984, 1987). However, the true numbers of female abusers are not known, as organised abuse, in which there are many allegations about the involvement of women, has not received the same level of public or policy attention.

The *Diagnostic and Statistical Manual of Mental Disorders*, DSM-V (American Psychiatric Association, 2013) is a manual used to diagnose all mental illnesses. It underlines the fact that abnormal sexual preferences must involve physical harm and psychological distress to be diagnosed as a paraphilic disorder. The diagnosis should therefore indicate whether the individual is in a controlled environment preventing contact with others or if symptoms have been in remission for a minimum of five years without psychological distress.

A diagnosis of sexual sadism does not mean that the person with this condition accepts or understands their diagnosis. However, the term applies to both individuals who admit to their urges to inflict physical and psychological pain and to those who deny or disavow their actions. Unsurprisingly, there is a poorer treatment outcome for those who cannot accept the meaning or nature of their intentions.

We now move from mainstream understanding of sexual sadism to an understanding of perpetration and sexual sadism in organised criminal groups using ritualistic elements.

Ritual perpetrators: definitions and introduction

Ritual perpetrators in organised crime

In June 2008, I presented a paper at the Safeguarding London Children conference in which my colleague Aduale and I differentiated between spiritual abuse and ritual abuse: spiritual abuse is the use or misuse of a position of power, leadership, or control in which a child or adult is made to feel that they, their families, or those they love are doomed in this life and in an after-life if they do not follow unquestioningly what they are asked to say or do.

We contrasted this type of abuse with ritual abuse, describing the latter as abuse that involved children or adults in physical, psycho-logical, or sexual abuse associated with repeated activities ("ritual") which purport to relate the abuse to contexts of a religious, magical, or supernatural kind, in which a child or adult is made to feel that they, their families, or those they love are doomed in this life and in an after-life if they do not follow unquestioningly what they are asked to say or do.

If we take away the religious or pseudo-religious excuses or veils for sadism that groups of abusers apply (either out of true belief or to create greater fear in the victims), we find that the most common alle-gations made by survivors include murder, infanticide, enforced preg-nancy and abortion, oral, anal, and vaginal rape, bestiality, asphyxia, binding, necrophilia, grievous bodily harm, being made to drink blood or semen, and eat non-food substances such as insects, faeces, and so on. This list is validated cross-culturally and internationally (Rutz et al., 2007). It also bears a startling resemblance to Krafft-Ebings's findings, as described earlier.

Indeed, if we look at the behaviours of serial killers and rapists, we find similar lists. Sadly, the two groups have not been able to be com-pared in a straightforward way previously because the organised abuse perpetrators in the United Kingdom are protected through the fear they engender in their victims, and societal disbelief.

In clinical practice, we usually learn about the sexual sadism of ritual abuse perpetrators through the impact on their victims, the internalisa-tion of such sadistic states of mind in the victims, the occasional encoun-ters of the victims with their perpetrators, and the nature and details of disclosures and comparison with similar groups.

A perpetrator comes for treatment

This, sadly, is the smallest category. Although victims who come seek-ing treatment have often been forced to perpetrate, and therefore are "victim-perpetrators", they are not characterologically interested in such acts and commit them only under duress. In the United Kingdom, we are more likely to see a perpetrator of sexual sadism if they deliberately accompany a family member to therapy to show their presence and power. Whilst we can consider clinically the possibility that they are curious about a treatment process for themselves, we do not have any evidence to corroborate this. However, comments by victims as to the meaning of their attendance offer a different interpretation.

Cult perpetrators who are dealt with in court have usually been sentenced for rape or grievous bodily harm as, in the United Kingdom, ritual crime is not a separate offence. Referrals from prison services concerning harrowing behaviour or disclosures of a ritualistic kind are usually highly confidential.

Additionally, where the perpetrator has a dissociative identity disorder, the lack of professional training and understanding means that the evidence held within a perpetrator alter could be lost. A perpetrator alter is an introject resulting from a dissociative split following a traumatic incident. What is different about such alters, as opposed to more usual alters formed totally for protection of the self, as a creative defensive act, is that they are totally modelled on an external abuser. This is very different to a defensive alter who identifies with abusive outsiders for survival. In other words, the therapist who has chosen to work with victims in a non-forensic setting finds they are working with the most chilling kind of perpetrator.

The intrapsychic impact on the victim of sexual sadism

To preserve confidentiality, I present a clinical illustration of treatment with a young woman who is an amalgam of several people I worked with in the 1990s.

A young woman who had been abused by her family had internalised their hatred of her, identified with it, and punished and damaged her own body mercilessly and with sexual sadism. At the end of an assessment session, having virulently stated why no-one would ever be able to help and what appalling treatment she had received throughout her life, she left fifteen minutes early, slamming the door so violently that the whole room shook and a therapist in the next-door room came out to see what had happened. I sat shell-shocked and then worried. I was sure a further communication would happen.

It did. Exactly at the point when the assessment would have ended, the phone rang. It was her. Her voice was laced with triumph and sexual excitement. "Hello there. Thought I'd catch you. Waiting for me were you, pathetic wanker. Well, I'm sitting in the carpark opposite and I just smashed a really nice bottle and I am going to cut my wrists until I die, the blood is already pouring out." I dialled 999 and got an ambulance there, and she was taken to hospital.

That kind of experience taught me a lot. The thought of depending on or caring about a woman therapist who might be able to offer something was so dangerous that I had to be hurt and controlled. She did not attack me directly. She let me sit and worry about her being hurt, a form of symbolic long-distance sadism. At the same time, she sexualised hurting herself as a defence against the terror of engulfment, on the one hand, or of abandonment, on the other. It was no accident that she left before the end of the assessment.

This process shows itself most clearly through the nature of the perpetrator and victim introjects in dissociative identity disorder. A clinical study on patients alleging ritual abuse in the United Kindgom found that one-third of the alleged victims had a diagnosis of dissociative identity disorder (Hale & Sinason, 1998).

Dissociative identity disorder (DID)

This is described in DSM-V (American Psychiatric Association, 2013) as the disruption of identity characterised by two or more distinct personality states, which may be described in some cultures as an experience of being "possessed". The disruption of marked discontinuity in sense of self and sense of agency is accompanied by related alterations in affect, behaviour, consciousness, memory, perception, cognition, and/or sensory-motor functioning. These signs and symptoms may be observed by others or reported by the individual.

The intrapsychic impact on the DID victim who comes for treatment

According to Sachs and Galton (2008), DID is a forensic condition in that ninety per cent of those with this diagnosis are likely to have experienced childhood sexual abuse (Fonagy & Target, 1995). In other words,

DID is the result of a crime, and that is one of the reasons why it evokes such intense responses.

When the experienced trauma reaches a level that exceeds the child's capacity to see or know, fragmentation of narrative and memory is a defence that allows some respite. Whilst the alters or fragmented states all contain something of the unique child who was so hurt, there also, of course, are present the traces of the adults who hurt them. Sometimes, in some systems, the power of those modelled on outside abusers means they are almost a replica, and the therapist and other alter personalities experience through these attacks the imprint of the original abuser.

I have written of internal murder (Sinason, 2008). In this, a perpetrator alter or victim-perpetrator alter attacks a victim alter, whom they perceive as a separate human being, with the aim of murder. To the outside world, this can look like severe self-injury. However, I consider it as a different process akin to murder. The alter assaulted does not return and is internally perceived as having been killed. More recently (Morton & Sinason, 2015), I have been researching what we call "quaternary structural dissociation", in which the perpetrator alter has been deliberately created by the abusive group rather than being a self-created defence. Internal sexual sadism also exists in which different emotional personalities, usually child states, who hold the worst trauma memories, are held in thrall, isolated, controlled, humiliated, mocked, and sexually attacked. Trying to deal with the internal sadist is possibly as hard as dealing with the external one.

As Breitenbach explains:

> A perpetrator threatens to kill a victim during a simple rape if she doesn't say the words that he tells her to say, words that insult and humiliate the victim as she begs to be tortured and abused. This experience can leave the perpetrator and victim intact, inside a multiple system. The perpetrator is dissociated from any feelings except sexual pleasure when humiliating and hurting others inside who, s/he has been taught, needs to be hurt.
>
> (Breitenbach, 2015, p. 44)

The impact on the psychotherapeutic relationship

With systematic abuse that has extended throughout childhood and almost into middle age, there is a greater likelihood of more sadistic internal perpetrators. The shame and guilt at being involved in abusive relationships increases with age, especially when the victim has also been made to perpetrate too. This leads to more attacks on the therapeutic relationship and indicates a far harder transference and countertransference experience for the therapist. In this situation, the therapist has to deal with a feeling of being controlled and punished and held accountable for any error, however slight. Again, as Breitenbach explains:

> The cost of such a relationship is also that personal injury, humiliation, accusations and insinuations as well as betrayal or the allegation of betrayal will enter into the therapy relationship. Our efforts will be reassessed, given different meanings; apparent events that never occurred in that way will suddenly arise such as distortions of what happened in therapy and new scenarios that make the therapist appear sadistic.
>
> (Breitenbach, 2015, p. 44)

Comparison with similar forensic perpetrator samples

With over twenty-five years' experience of working with this population, and having had the privilege of hearing over a thousand victims and survivors of this form of abuse, we can now make some comments on the context as we hear it. Patients from all over the United Kingdom, and internationally too, provide similar accounts of lived experience at the hands of organised crime/cult masters and mistresses.

We can learn more about this group of sadists hiding in plain sight by comparing them with groups of others who commit the same crimes, and I shall start with the disturbing parallels in the comparison.

What we have found (Hale & Sinason, 1994) is that perpetrators of organised abuse cannot bear separation and loss and seek to deny it and disavow it. In doing this, they risk losing all hope of the good-enough mother. The choice is to kill the longed-for woman in the actual mother (or stand-in) or to allow her to stay alive through controlling her, making her suffer, and gaining arousal from it. Indeed, separation anxiety is so severe through the lack of any secure attachment that creating a hell-on-earth for their victims is possibly a way of bolstering a needed belief in endless time.

Through the patterns of abusers which have been imprinted and internalised in their victims, we find that acts that would be considered extremely violent and criminal in ordinary society are part of "normal" ordinary life for such groups. Special occasions, dates, ceremonies, punishments provide the excuse for extending criminal boundaries further in the need to evacuate all mental content. The Marquis de Sade's prison fantasies of isolated impregnable stately homes where libertines could increase their depravity until murder was all that was left were not only literally true for the appalling state of the Bastille, but also true of the domestic home where ritual abuse occurs, and true also of all the venues that host sadistic abuse.

By torturing together, organised groups of cult sadists share the guilt, shame, and terror, making the small child who longs for and needs and deserves love and safety the receptacle of all their sadism and perversion. Trauma-bonding, coercive practices, terror, and manipulation of attachment needs keep their victims silenced, often becoming identified with their aggressors, and consequently trying out on their own bodies what was done to them. Those who manage to leave and escape such groups can find it extremely hard to find their own sexual identity. They never learned to have a sexual feeling that was not encouraged or created by a cult sadist. Their bodies and all orifices were owned by the group.

As Fromm has delineated, the

> core of sadism … is the passion to have absolute and unrestricted control over living beings, … whether an animal, child, a man or a woman. To force someone to endure pain or humiliation without being able to defend himself is one of the manifestations of absolute control, but it is by no means the only one. The person who has complete control over another living being makes this being into his thing, his property, while he becomes the other being's god.
>
> (Fromm, 1973, pp. 383–384)

Of course, there can be cult masters who do not wish to see the suffering of the victim as they wish them to hide it, and there are psychopaths too who do not derive pleasure in the suffering.

Dietz et al. (1990) provided a descriptive study of thirty sexually sadistic criminals. All were men, and all had intentionally tortured their victims in order to arouse themselves. Their crimes often involved careful planning, the selection of strangers as victims, approaching the victim under a pretext, participation of a partner, beating victims, restraining victims and holding them captive, sexual bondage, anal rape, forced fellatio, vaginal rape, foreign object penetration, telling victims to speak particular words in a degrading manner, murder or serial killings (most often by strangulation), concealing victims' corpses, recording offences, and keeping personal items belonging to victims. While committing these offences, forty-three per cent were married. The nine who were incestuously involved with their children comprised thirty per cent of the total sample, but sixty per cent of the fifteen subjects who had children.

A significant number of sadistic perpetrators have an interest in police uniforms and in police protocols. Interest in police paraphernalia is important as so many cult sadists either pretend to be and dress up as policeman, or include policemen.

The most striking difference between the causes of death in sadistic murders and the distribution of causes of death among murder victims generally is the relatively high proportion of asphyxia (sixty-one per cent) and the relatively low proportion of gunshot wounds (twenty-five per cent). This also fits with our understanding of the tortures that cult victims have reported. Gunshot indicates a direct wish to kill, which is very different to the wish to control and torture that strangulation allows.

Another link with organised crime perpetrators is that there is a shared hatred/fear of the female vagina, and the focus is on the mouth and anus for both male and female victims.

The female victims had a similar background: seventy-five per cent had been psychologically abused, and in adulthood fifty per cent had previously been involved in abusive relationships, which shows a process of re-enactment whereby early relational matrices are replicated in later life.

Many of the dynamics used in other kinds of "brainwashing" or "mind control" seem to be used in this context. Not only does the sadist isolate the children and women from other intimate relationships, but he also physically, mentally, sexually, and spiritually degrades and humiliates with small "rewards" for compliance.

This intermeshing of attachment with perversion raises complex questions concerning criminal responsibility. As I have mentioned with regard to Rosemary West, several female victims eventually became co-conspirators and co-perpetrators with the sadists in serious criminal activities. We need a law on duress to aid the cult victim to come forward without fear of imprisonment. In cults where victims have been forced to be perpetrators, this is even more important. How can these groups be broken up if the victims are in danger of being criminalised? Where does this leave the victim-perpetrator, and where does it leave the perpetrator? If there is no way out for the sexual sadist except imprisonment, then that in itself will enhance the criminal escalation.

Those who choose to come to therapy are already in a completely different category. It means they are daring to deal with the unbearable shame that comes from being used in these ways. However, for the sociopathic sadists, trapped in their endless cycles, who use children and vulnerable adults as their dustbins, we need to remove the mystique of religious mumbo-jumbo from them and show far more clearly how they fit into line with other criminals. Given the fact that satiation and unbearable mental content drives cult sadists to continue with their attacks and increase them, the lack of success in dealing with and reporting this is even more serious. Reporting to the police about such an individual or group is like trying to leave the mafia. It is not enough to merely offer a new home.

Sexual sadists from organised abuse rarely come openly for treatment. Often, as with Cyril Smith MP and the entertainer and fundraiser Jimmy Savile, both high-profile figures in the United Kingdom, they are publicly exposed only after their death. That tells us of the fear they evoke. Increasing numbers of victims are coming forward, but that is only the start. However, if my hypothesis is correct in the way that such perpetrators follow the pattern of serial killers who are also sexual sadists then there is even more clinical and forensic need for attention.

The perpetrators have an unbearable dilemma. They cannot bear what is in their minds, but each act to relieve their mental anguish brings untold pain to their victims, society, and onto themselves. Societal disavowal of their actions leaves them hidden in their Sadean palaces or hiding in plain sight. In plain sight, we watch the deterioration and destruction of children and adults.

Acknowledgements

With particular thanks to Amita Sehgal for her rigorous and helpful editing, which, in some places, more merits the term of second author. Her editorial questions also showed where further explanation was needed.

References

American Psychiatric Association (2013). *Diagnostic and Statistical Manual of Mental Disorders*, Fifth Edition. Arlington, VA: American Psychiatric Publishing.

Beeger, P., Berner, W., Bolterauer, J., Gutierrez, K., & Berger, K. (1999). Sadistic personality disorder in sex offenders. *Journal of Personality Disorder, 13*: 175–186.

Breitenbach, G. (2015). *Inside Views from the Dissociated Worlds of Extreme Violence.* London: Karnac.

Dietz, P. E., Hazelwood, R., & Warren, J. (1990). The sexually sadistic criminal and his offenses. *Bulletin of the American Academy of Psychiatry and Law, 18*: 167.

Fromm, E. (1973). *The Anatomy of Human Destructiveness.* Minnesota: Fawcett Crest Publishers.

Glasser, M. (1978). The role of the superego in exhibitionism. *International Journal of Psychoanalytic Psychotherapy, 7*: 333–352.

Glasser, M. (1986). Identification and its vicissitudes as observed in the perversions. *International Journal of Psycho-Analysis, 67*: 9–17.

Glasser, M. (1996). Aggression and sadism in the perversions. In: I. Rosen (Ed.), *Sexual Deviation* (pp. 279–299). Oxford: Oxford University Press.

Glasser, M. (1998). On violence: a preliminary communication. *The International Journal of Psycho-Analysis, 79*: 887–902.

Hale, R., & Sinason, V. (1998). *Clinical Outcome of Ritual Abuse Study.* Portman Clinic Formal Press Release. Tavistock and Portman Clinics, London.

Hazelwood, R., Dietz, P., & Warren, J. (1992). The criminal sexual sadist. *Federal Bureau Investigation Law Enforcement Bulletin, 61*: 12–20.

Hill, A., Habermann, N., Berner, W., & Briken, P. (2006). Sexual sadism and sadistic personality disorder in sexual homicide. *Journal of Personality Disorders, 20*: 671–684.

Krafft-Ebing, R. von (1886). *Psychopathia Sexualis.* New York: Stein and Day, 1989.

Morton, J., & Sinason, V. (2014). *Quaternary Structural Dissociation.* International Society for the Study of Trauma and Dissociation, Thirty-First Conference, 25–27 October. Long Beach, USA.

Rutz, C., Overkamp, B., Karriker, W., & Becker, T. (2007). *Extreme Abuse Survey Project.* Accessed at: http://www.extreme-abuse-survey.net

Sachs, A., & Galton, G. (2008). *Forensic Aspects of Dissociative Identity Disorder.* London: Karnac.

Sinason, V. (2008). When murder strikes inside. In: A. Sachs & G. Galton (Eds.), *Forensic Aspects of Dissociative Identity Disorder* (pp. 100–107). London: Karnac.

Weinberg, T. S., Williams, C. J., & Moser, C. (1984). The social constituents of sadomasochism. *Social Problems, 31*: 379–389.

Weinberg, T. S. (1987). Sadomasochism in the United States: a review of recent sociological literature. *Journal of Sex Research, 23*: 50–69.

Welldon, E. V. (2011). *Playing with Dynamite: A Personal Approach to the Psychoanalytic Understanding of Perversions, Violence, and Criminality*. London: Karnac.

Welldon, E. V., & Van Velsen, C. (1997). *A Practical Guide to Forensic Psychotherapy*. London: Jessica Kingsley.

CHAPTER FIVE

Sadism and intellectual disability

Richard Curen

Introduction

In this chapter, I describe my work as a forensic disability psychotherapist with two men with intellectually disabilities. Forensic disability psychotherapy does not condone crime but focuses on illness and risk (Corbett, 2014). It aims to foster a psychodynamic understanding of offenders and contribute to their treatment. This helps the offender to acknowledge responsibility, thereby protecting the offender and society from perpetration of further crimes. Each of the two men I worked with presented with sadistic states of mind and both struggled to make sense of their sadistic preoccupations. Both men displayed a limited capacity for self-reflection and resorted to enacting sadistic fantasies in an attempt to seek respite from unbearable feelings of anxiety. I discuss my work within the wider theoretical context of sadism and present my experience of the challenges of working with intellectually disabled people with compulsive sadistic preoccupations.

All of the clinical material I describe has been carefully anonymised to protect confidentiality without losing the essence of the individuals' situations and the associated dynamics. I have either assessed or treated these individuals at Respond, which is a non-government organisation providing psychological assessment and treatment services for people with intellectual disabilities or autism.

Intellectual disability

Intellectual disability is a general term that refers to individuals who find it harder than others to learn, understand, and communicate. Other terms that are used to describe such an individual's situation include complex needs or high support needs. Intellectual disability is a lifelong condition that can have a significant impact on a person's life and that of their family. Many people with intellectual disability will require support to enable them to live as independently as possible (Holland, 2011).

Authors including Sinason (1992) and O'Driscoll (2009) have helped shine a light on the terms used to describe people with intellectual disabilities and how the terms have generally been used to shame and control, rather than to empower or foster self-actualisation. A psycho-analytic theory of intellectual disability developed by Alvarez (1992, 2012), Sinason (1992), and Symington (1992) has deepened our understanding of the internal worlds of people with intellectual disabilities and the application of psychodynamically informed treatment. Similarly, by focusing on perversion and forensic issues, Corbett (2014) has grounded and enhanced a new way of thinking about the aetiology and treatment of the intellectually disabled who have developed perverse solutions to intolerable sexual anxieties. By placing trauma and loss as an often neglected but fundamental area of attention in the lives of people with intellectual disabilities, Corbett (1996), Cottis (2009), Blackman (2013), and Frankish (2016) provide another cornerstone to understanding these core experiences and their manifestations in worrying behaviours.

A central aspect of working clinically with intellectually disabled people is understanding how different their lives may be to those in mainstream society, and how society may care for them and support their families. People with intellectual disabilities are often likely to have additional conditions such as autism, physical disabilities, challenging behaviours,[1] communication difficulties, self-injurious behaviour, epilepsy, or life-limiting disorders. The prevalence of mental health problems in people with intellectual disabilities is significantly higher than in the general population (Cooper et al., 2007). The range of people's abilities can vary hugely, with some people who have been identified as intellectually disabled being indistinguishable from those who have not been regarded as disabled. The disability may become obvious only once one gets to know the person well, and even then under specific circumstances, for example when they are feeling anxious.

At the other end of the spectrum would be those people regarded as having severe or profound intellectual disabilities, who may exhibit a varied range of characteristics, including dependence on others to provide basic support around feeding and personal care, difficulties in getting around unaided, and significant delays in reaching developmental milestones. Some people have limited communication skills and may have reduced control over speech, body language, and facial expressions. It should be remembered that a person's difficulty in expressing themselves does not reduce their wish to communicate. Similarly, someone's intellectual ability may have no bearing on their emotional range, so whilst some people may experience a full and complex range of emotions, they may lack the ability to communicate their experiences other than in rudimentary ways.

When we consider some of the more complex features of people with intellectual disabilities as a whole, we find there are some common themes:

1. The quality of their attachments are often significantly impacted by the stresses associated with growing up with disabilities.
2. They are more likely to be victims of sexual abuse and domestic violence (Euser et al., 2016; Mitra et al., 2011; Reiter et al., 2007; Spencer et al., 2005).
3. They often have deficits in their sexual development and in their ability to experiment sexually with peers (McCabe, 1993).
4. Society is often hostile towards them, resulting in many feeling isolated and marginalised.
5. Life feels demanding and challenging, leading to a desire to escape or disappear.

Alongside these limiting features, we find that some people, just as in the general population, and particularly as a response to trauma, deprivation, or violence in the home or within the community, may demonstrate sexual frustrations due to:

1. Limited sexual knowledge.
2. Often being closely supervised so that any sexual act is observed and then subjected to scrutiny.

3. Being more likely to be "discovered" when acting out sexually due to a lack of privacy or opportunities.
4. Being more impulsive, having fewer inhibitions, and a lack of understanding about the consequences on others of actions.
5. Finding it difficult to develop consenting peer relationships.
6. Lacking an erotic script that is socially acceptable.
7. Parents hoping that their child (even when physically an adult) will not develop sexual desires, and therefore avoid the complicated and anxiety-provoking arena of sex and relationships.

Sadism

Freud's (1905d) understanding of perversion developed when he started to think of it as a defensive function against the reality of the Oedipus complex. From this, we can see that what is perverted is knowledge of psychic reality. The denial of reality uses sadistic control of the object that leads to a way of relating that is sadomasochistic, perverse, and based on a corruption of facts about other people. The central dynamic in the sexually perverse act is the corruption of the other's mind by corrupting truth and reality. Sadism is therefore a perversion that has its roots in infantile sexuality. Building on Freud's theories, Stoller places aggression at the core of sexual perversions:

> Think of the perversions ... in each is found—in gross form or hidden—hostility, revenge, triumph and a dehumanised object. Before even scratching the surface, we can see that someone harming someone else is a main feature in most of these conditions.
> (Stoller, 1976, p. 9)

It follows then that the goal of the sadist is to harm, control, and keep at a "safe" distance an object that is forced to respond in a way that brings temporary respite from feelings of anxiety and isolation. Violence, actual or the threat of it, is the way in which control is exercised. Fonagy (2003) writes that violence that is acted out on others attests to a failure in negotiating infancy and to a likely lack of primitive containment. For many of us, having murderous thoughts is simply a part of being human; however, almost all of us are able to have the thoughts without needing to, or feeling like we have to, put them into action.

Sadism can be viewed as a "sexualised" solution to the problem of not being able to mentalise, that is, a person's lack of capacity for reflection. The difference between those who act out their aggression/ perversion via sadism and those who do not is often connected to failures in containment at early developmental stages. Some people are able to transform perverse solutions into fantasies; however, others do not have the capacity to do this and therefore need to enact them (Morgan & Ruszczynski, 2007).

Sadism and intellectual disability

The presence of sexual perversions indicates that there might be unresolved or un-worked-through developmental stages, and Freud (1905d) wrote that sexual perversions are a deviation in the aim of the sexual instinct. The sadist needs the other to suffer but also needs to keep the other alive in order to fulfil the aggressive enactment. If we apply this dynamic to society, we can see that there is a need to maintain an illusion of homeostasis, with the intellectually disabled becoming the receptacle for others' disavowed feelings of inferiority and of the fear of becoming disabled. Examples can be seen in enactments of disability hate crime and disability-related harassment, which, in the extreme, result in individuals being kept and treated as despised pets, tortured, and occasionally murdered.

In this chapter, I wish to emphasise that it is important to hold in mind the pathological tendencies for intolerance and aggression that coexist in both the individual and in society as a whole. This also applies to the family environment, where the child can become the receptacle of the family's projections. For example, I came to know of a young man of seventeen who was charged with attempted rape of a younger girl. When his father was asked about his thoughts on the matter, he replied that it cannot have been that serious, but that it was simply yet another example of his son not even getting that right. I was struck by this father's emasculation and hatred of his disabled child, and of what a profound effect this kind of attitude must have had on the young man.

Sexual perversions, including sadism, can be viewed as temporary solutions to developmental struggles that children and adolescents have to negotiate. I suggest that there are at least four reasons why a sexual perversion may emerge in individuals with intellectual disabilities. These are:

1. Defences against remembering poor parental relationships, including neglect or abuse.

2. Defences against further instability of sexual identity—in order to avoid the emergence and instability of a fixed gender identity.
3. Defences against loneliness, anxiety, shame, or anger, as in a retreat from anxiety and unpleasant feelings.
4. Defences against adapting to the demands of life, like an erotic hideaway that has an almost psychotic feel to it, but is also a defence against "a breakdown in the defensive shield" (Sinason, 1992, p. 23).

These defences delay or put off forever the integration of what are in reality difficult and problematic areas that need to be negotiated in order to live in a more integrated way. For people with intellectual disabilities, it is essential that there is enough support in their environment in order for them to manage the very significant demands that are part of their everyday lives. According to the Equality and Human Rights Commission's report into Disability-Related Harassment (2011), people with intellectual disabilities experience hate crime, disability-related harassment, and other violent and hateful projections from society. These must have a profound effect on individuals and their families, and sometimes this may be projected back. Examples of the way society can view disability appear in the tabloids reporting on celebrity pregnancies and the fear of having a child with disabilities,[2] and also the regular stories about medical "progress" in the battle against Down's syndrome.[3]

Problems can arise in our understanding of sadism when a pattern of behaviour that has previously been masochistic transforms and flips into sadism. The sense that a person is simply hurting themselves and therefore is not a risk to anyone else can quickly be turned on its head when the violence is turned outward instead of inwards. As people with intellectual disabilities often have much closer involvement with families and paid carers, a tension can exist in the way that sadism is recognised and addressed. Carers can struggle to see that sadistic behaviours are communications connected to states of mind that are powerfully being projected onto others in the environment.

One example of this was the case of a man I worked with who was in his early sixties with a mild intellectual disability, and who was referred for treatment after years of using auto-asphyxiation as a masturbatory aid. There was no history of violence to anyone else, and he would have sexual relations with sex workers who would often dominate and humiliate him. During this time, his elderly parents could no longer care for him and he moved into supported living. In the care home, he would regularly set up scenes in which he was auto-asphyxiating, for staff to discover him. Whilst the staff managed these situations, very few attempts were made at understanding what this man was trying to communicate to those around him. Subsequently, he attacked a woman in the street by putting a bag over her head in order to asphyxiate her. He was arrested and charged, and a compulsory hospital admission followed. It was then that a concerted effort was made to try to understand the roots of his behaviour. Of interest was his idealisation of his mother, who was observed to treat him in critical, disdainful, and mocking ways. The attack on the woman could then start to be seen as the possible expression of unconscious feelings of aggression, anxiety, and hatred towards his mother that he was unable to express consciously.

Another man, aged thirty, with a mild intellectual disability would ask women in the community if they would give him a "wedgie".[4] He also joked about his middle name being "humiliation". This was an attempt to create a smokescreen in order to disarm and be jocular about something that was deeply upsetting and traumatising. As the requests for wedgies were made in a lighthearted way, they could easily be laughed off as a bit of a joke. Occasionally, he would find women who would do this to him and, when this happened, it would lead to an increase in other more obviously aggressive and sadistic behaviours. These included threats of physical violence towards, and violent attacks on, support staff and other residents in his group home. In this case, the wedgies can be understood as expressions of an infantile sexuality that seemed to have three main features: first, the act of giving someone a wedgie stimulates the genitals and the anus; second, the act has an element of humiliation or masochism as the strength required to give someone a wedgie could physically injure them; and third, the act is similar in nature to castration as the male genitals can become squeezed back into the body. Interestingly, this man seemed to have no wish for a reciprocal sexual relationship; instead, his interest was solely focused on his own masochistic pleasure and humiliation.

Sadistic behaviours that become wrapped up in a person's everyday presentation to the extent that these become almost indistinguishable from it are harder to spot. In care homes, support staff may find it particularly hard to recognise sadistic acting out and can tend to it pass off as simply "challenging behaviour". For example, a man in his early twenties with autism and a moderate intellectual disability was living in a group care home. Following two incidents when he exposed himself to members of the public, he was placed under supervision for all subsequent outings. However, when in the house and over a long period of time, he would hug staff as they arrived or left at shift changeover times. Some of the staff allowed this behaviour whereas others deemed it to be inappropriate. As time went on, the hugs became tighter, longer-lasting, and would end with a very low-key attempt to hurt the member of staff, for example with a slap or a punch. Whilst these incidents did not constitute serious physical assaults, they became a way in which he had started to "torture" the staff. The physical contact slowly became harder and more obvious until the behaviour was eventually halted when all staff agreed upon a consistent way of greeting and saying goodbye to him that did not involve physical contact.

Case examples

In order to further develop and explore the links between sadism and intellectual disability, I will focus on clinical material from two individuals. For both of them, fantasies of eating, digesting, and controlling others had become the means of expressing their sadistic fantasies and thoughts. The fear of being eaten or of there not being enough goodness to take in links to the earliest experiences and phantasies related to breast-feeding, and of devouring and being devoured.

Case study one

Luke (not his real name) was a fifty-four-year-old male with a moderate intellectual disability and autism, living in a small supported living service. Previously, he had lived alone with his mother. His father had been violent to Luke's mother until she moved into a refuge when Luke was seven years old. His disability became more obvious as he got older, as he struggled to communicate effectively, was socially awkward, and unable to make and maintain friendships of any kind apart from with his mother. In adolescence and early adulthood, he was quick to perceive others, women in particular, as having disrespected him, and he would often respond in retaliatory ways. The retaliations would include written letters referring to his sexual preoccupations, and these were often aggressive and somewhat bizarre and unsettling for the intended reader. As the content of his letters started to include descriptions of sexual violence towards babies, Luke was referred to Respond by his psychiatrist for a forensic risk assessment (or risk analysis) in order to evaluate his risk to others, but also his vulnerability to abuse and his suitability for treatment.

Luke was escorted to Respond's clinic for the twelve-session assessment (designed to maximise opportunities to build a trusting working relationship) that included a range of assessments designed to explore various topics using multiple methods such as questionnaires, hypothetical scenarios, a sex-education manual designed by people with intellectual disabilities for people with intellectual disabilities, as well as using psychoanalytic concepts of transference and countertransference.

Luke attended all of the assessment sessions on time and seemed interested and engaged with the process. However, he appeared lacking in affect and reflective capacity, and demonstrated an autistic way of thinking. For example, when asked specific questions relating to his sexual knowledge and fantasies, he responded concretely; when asked to imagine having a partner, he responded "but I don't have a partner". It seemed hard for him to imagine events that had not already happened.

Luke's memories of his childhood included being breast-fed and having his nappy changed. He talked about his mother and father and how he wished things had been different between them. Luke had found school difficult as he had experienced lots of bullying. He described often being punched, slapped, and having his head put down the loo. Luke recalled an incident aged six years old when his mother had asked his father to clear away porn magazines that his father had left lying around the home. Eventually, his mother herself got rid of these, but not before Luke's father had shown Luke a picture of a vagina and an anus. Luke remembers this as a moment of great significance in his life, one that profoundly affected the way he made sense of the world of sex and relationships.

Assessing the extent of knowledge and understanding of sexual matters is often key to treating people who have developed harmful sexual interests in the absence of any prior sexual experience. Luke claimed a lack of any previous sexual experiences with another person. Given his age, his sexual knowledge seemed limited and immature. During the assessment, Luke presented with limited basic understanding of heterosexual sex and how babies are made. For example, he knew that the man puts his penis inside the woman's vagina but did not know that may lead to pregnancy. Luke thought that babies simply grew in the mother's belly and there was no need for fertilisation. Luke's belief in an "immaculate" conception seems to suggest a fantasy where there is no potent and aggressive father but, instead, an imagined mother–baby dyad that has no beginning or end—an infinite blissful union, unthreatened by a potentially castrating father.

During the assessment, Luke said that he had never had a sexual partner, he would like to have one in the future but he was too young. When asked why he thought he was too young, he said that his mother had told him this. This seemed to indicate a strong maternal influence over him, with the mother's attendant anxieties about Luke getting close to someone other than her. Interestingly, in one of the sessions, Luke said that his mother was concerned that the assessment was "teaching" him too much about sex.

Luke expressed a strong interest in coprophilia (that is, perverse sexual gratification involving faeces and defecation). He said once he had shown a girlfriend how to wipe herself whilst she was on the toilet, and described how he would "help her out". He also described a desire to smell women's anuses, and how he wanted to be able to persuade a woman to let him do this to her. This seemed to demonstrate a sexual fantasy with a strong erotic charge, although Luke did not describe any past or future sexual enjoyment associated with this activity. However, inherent in the acts he described there was an element of humiliation, either of himself or of the other.

The referral letter described Luke having a long history of writing letters to various people, usually females, whom he felt had disrespected, humiliated, or bullied him. He said that writing the letters made his angry feelings go away, and sometimes he would leave the letters in phone boxes for people to find. The assessment focused on a specific letter that Luke had left in the disabled toilet of a library to be found by the female worker, whom, he felt, had humiliated him by looking at him in a way that suggested to him that she thought he was fat and ugly. The long letter described how he wanted to put his penis inside the anus of a tiny little female baby until she bled and died. Then this baby would give birth to another baby girl whom he would proceed to anally rape and impregnate before she too died and produced another female baby. He described repeating anal rape on this new baby girl, who would also die and give birth to yet another baby girl who would scream at being anally raped, and so on.

The cycle of anal rape, pregnancy, murder, and birth provides an interesting insight into a part of Luke's mind that was not directly available in the assessment sessions. In Luke's letter-writing, there is a strong emphasis on babies being the result of anal sex. These letters not only revealed Luke's confused ideas about birth, sex, and death, but also provided a vehicle for him to express his suppressed primitive drives and desires through a stream of never-ending sadistic fantasies of control and punishment. His behaviour could then be understood as an unconscious cry for help in order to make sense of complex existential drives that had become perverted.

People with intellectual disabilities tend to imagine that they are the product of a sexual connection that was violent, that is, "bad" sex. Sinason (1992) and Wolfensberger (1987) describe how patients with intellectual disabilities harbour unconscious phantasies of their parents having caused their disability through a destructive union. Similarly, some people may imagine that in their mother's womb there was no more goodness left for them. Corbett (2014) has described how some people with intellectual disabilities he has treated have imagined they shared their mother's womb with a twin baby whom they killed off out of violent greed to have the womb all to themselves. They imagine the destroyed baby would have been the non-disabled child had it not been for their destructive violence towards it.

Luke's sexual development seemed to have become arrested at an early stage, probably in a pre-genital developmental phase, as much of his fascination was to do with eating, faeces, and anuses. There were also links to being humiliated and degraded, or doing this to others, that point towards sadistic tendencies, that is, he did not know how to be with another person sexually and seemed stuck in a world of low self-esteem, shame, and little or no sexual gratification. Luke's fascination with faeces demonstrates a profound difficulty in understanding and assimilating the true nature of relationships and of a mature sexuality. What this meant was that Luke was deeply affected by feelings of shame, and he used grandiosity and perverse retreats in order to avoid these feelings.

Finally, the assessment report recommended that Luke needed long-term psychotherapeutic treatment if he were ever to come to terms with his desires and start to move into a more mature way of being in the world. However, in the current situation the risk to others was unknown, and only a long period of treatment might provide him with an opportunity to develop taking pleasure in ordinary, everyday experiences, and to understand the meaning of his perverse thoughts.

The overarching experience of working with Luke and of being in the room with him was one of stasis. Over the twelve weeks of the assessment, unlike with most people, there was very little change in terms of Luke's engagement, which remained very concrete and at times awkward. The assessor took the case to supervision regularly during the assessment period, and each time the transference and countertransference experiences were discussed. Corbett (2014) writes about "the disability transference", and in particular what is often experienced in the assessment and treatment of forensic disability patients:

> Being in the presence of a patient with a disability forces us into an
> encounter with those parts of our own psyche that resonate with
> notions of lack and loss ... our thoughts cluster around the missing
> cognitions in an attempt to both reassemble what is missing and to
> imagine how we would live with such a lacuna.
>
> (Corbett, 2014, p. 79)

The assessor described feelings of frustration and of seemingly losing their way during the sessions. This attested to the countertransference phenomena experienced with so many patients like Luke, particularly in the assessment process where there is some pressure to come up with understandings and explanations that fill in the gaps rather than allow for opportunities for realisations and connections to emerge. Patients such as Luke, with his sadistic phantasies, projected a false self that was content and seemingly unknowing of the impact on those people to whom he addressed his letters. The temptation to provide the knowledge by filling in the gaps so that Luke came to really know and understand what he had done was often overpowering and had to be disentangled in the supervision before it could be addressed in the assessment sessions. The impulse in the assessor to get through Luke's defences and to "reason" with him about the "unreason" of his actions was contained in the supervision where this could be talked about and unpicked.

Post-assessment, Luke started weekly forensic psychotherapy sessions with a Respond therapist, and after nearly two years of at times challenging treatment the letter-writing stopped and Luke began to become more aware of his sadistic phantasies and their function in protecting him from deep-seated dissatisfaction with his lack of a sexual partner, fears about death and dying, and his life as a disabled person. Hollins and Grimer's (1998) idea of there being three secrets present in disability psychotherapy—sex, death, and the disability itself—provides another firm foundation in providing forensic disability psychotherapy, alongside Corbett's (2014) concept of disability transference and Welldon's (1988, 2011) ideas about perversion. Symington's (1992) thoughts on hatred in the countertransference with disabled patients and the way that projective identification works are also useful tools in the work with this group of patients, who can evoke feelings of rejection, anger, and denial that must be worked through in order to access a relationally based transformative means of at least attempting to facilitate change.

Case study two

Peter (not his real name) was referred to Respond by his psychologist due to concerns about his sadistic fantasies around female celebrities. His main fantasy was about making a soup out of these women and then eating it. He believed that in the process of eating their bodies, he would then be able to take over what he described as their "powers". These fantasised powers were related to an ability he felt some women had that made them perceive him as weak and vulnerable and not a "proper man".

Peter was twenty-nine and lived independently with another man with intellectual disabilities. Peter had a borderline intellectual disability, cerebral palsy, and Marfan syndrome that meant he had some difficulty with speech and was also very tall and had developed a stoop. He always looked down at the ground when he was standing and talking to others, and even when sitting he avoided eye contact with others around him. He was also referred for treatment due to concerns about his risk to women; he would sometimes deliberately bump into them in the street or swear at them when he was walking closely past them. Over the years, Peter had bought himself many pairs of women's shoes, which he used to masturbate over and into. In the treatment, he quickly started to talk about his fantasies about bringing some "sexy and stylish" women's shoes from his collection to the clinic and leaving them at reception while he was with his psychotherapist. His fantasy was that a female member of staff would look into the bag and be consumed with jealous feelings because she did not own these shoes.

At the end of a session, he imagined he would triumphantly pick up the bag and take the shoes back home with him. Most exciting for Peter was the idea that the member of staff's peek into the bag was itself a punishable act that would result in the "sacking" of the member of staff.

Peter had a cleaning job in a busy health centre and felt that the sight of attractive women on a daily basis fed his fantasies of violence and aggression. He would often follow women down the corridors and gesticulate behind them. Work was felt by him to be a source of frustration, where he felt confronted by women, but he also felt that if he were to leave his job, he would lose his independence and would need to rely on his family and particularly on his mother's support. Peter was in a situation similar to a double bind, in that to leave his job might have reduced the need for sadism but equally he feared the loss of self-esteem and the imagined disappointment of his parents would lead to other sadistic thoughts and fantasies. Work made him less dependent on his parents but also provided fuel for his fantasies and brought him into close proximity to women whom he felt despised him and made him feel like shit.

The treatment with Peter took place over five years, with attempts by the referrers to refer him to local services, as he had to rely upon the financial and practical support of his parents in order to get him to his sessions. He became very attached to the clinic and would often say that without his treatment he would have to kill himself. Peter would often talk about having suicidal thoughts, and towards the end of the treatment these increased to such a level that the team started talking about the possibility of a voluntary admission to a psychiatric unit. Following an incident in which Peter had "bumped into" a woman in the street because he didn't like the way she had looked at him, plus another incident in which he had slashed the tyres of a car that belonged to a woman he "didn't like", Peter was admitted into a psychiatric unit, where he subsequently suffered a mental collapse.

Discussion

The psychotherapy treatment provided Peter with an opportunity to re-enact the sadistic ways of relating that he used to control and manipulate others in his environment. Just like with Luke, phenomena such as splitting, projective identification, and relating in sadistic ways to others often emerge in the forensic treatment of people with intellectual disabilities. The role of the forensic disability psychotherapist is to tune into the manifestations of these phenomena in the transference and countertransference experiences both in the consulting room and being played out across the patient's network, that is, in families and amongst careers and professionals. For Peter, there was pleasure derived from the experience of bringing his perversion into the room for analysis. What this represented was a partial wish for the perversion to be at least shared, explored, and its stranglehold on him diminished. I also believe that the sadistic dynamic that Luke attempted to recreate in the consulting room was evident from the way he would point out what he perceived to be my struggles with intimacy, particularly with the female members of staff in the clinic. Luke would wonder aloud about how he thought the members of staff whom he detested also detested me. Therefore a sadomasochistic loop between myself, the staff, and Luke was attempted that would fit in with is perverse way of perceiving those around him—wanting to be in control and yet having no control. I strongly felt that Luke's sadism was what held him together and staved off an earlier breakdown.

Conclusion

Society tends to devalue the unintelligent and the disabled, and by association their families. Some families and individuals have the resources within them and around them with which to counter this attack, but they are the exception. People in need of help and support can often be left to fend for themselves, and when they ask for help can be made to feel like a drain on already overstretched resources.

The intersection of intellectual disability and sadism is one that continues to throw up new ways in which individuals try to gain mastery over unconscious processes that provide respite from unbearable feelings of anxiety. Welldon (1996) describes a circular motion of perversion that has anxiety at its centre driving it forward. Corbett (2014) adds to this the anxiety that is central to the experience of growing up with an intellectual disability, as a personification of brokenness and all that society would wish to cast out. For people like Luke and Peter, there is a reaching out to others for understanding and compassion, even though it is done in a way that might make one turn and run in the other direction. It is the role of clinicians—specifically the forensic disability psychotherapist—working with this patient group to try to contain and metabolise what is often deeply distasteful and designed to push people away. If we can make use of our transference and countertransference reactions, then there is hope for these patients to start to let go of these pathological ways of relating to others.

Notes

1. Challenging behaviour is often used as a euphemism for violent and aggressive behaviour that challenges professionals. There is a tendency, therefore, to manage or medicate a person until they stop being challenging and to avoid thinking about the behaviour as a communication of a state of mind that needs attention.
2. http://www.mirror.co.uk/tv/tv-news/katie-price-reveals-tried-abort-7981835
3. http://cphpost.dk/news/down-syndrome-heading-for-extinction-in-denmark.html
4. The definition of giving a wedgie is to pull someone's pants or underwear so far up that they become uncomfortably wedged between the cheeks of the person's bottom.

References

Alvarez, A. (1992). *Live Company: Psychoanalytic Psychotherapy with Autistic, Borderline, Deprived and Abused Children*. London: Routledge.
Alvarez, A. (2012). *The Thinking Heart: Three Levels of Psychoanalytic Therapy with Disturbed Children*. London: Routledge.
Blackman, N. A. (2013). The use of psychotherapy in supporting people with intellectual disabilities who have experienced bereavement. PhD dissertation, University of Hertfordshire, Hertford.
Cooper, S. A., Smiley, E., Morrison, J., Williamson, A., & Allan, L. (2007). Mental ill-health in adults with intellectual disabilities: prevalence and associated factors. *British Journal of Psychiatry, 190*: 27–35.
Corbett, A. (2014). *Disabling Perversions: Forensic Psychotherapy with People with Intellectual Disabilities*. London: Karnac.
Corbett, A., Cottis, T., & Morris, S. B. (1996). *Witnessing, Nurturing and Protesting: Therapeutic Responses to Sexual Abuse of People with Learning Disabilities*. London: David Fulton Publishers.
Cottis, T. (2009). *Intellectual Disability, Trauma and Psychotherapy*. London, New York: Routledge.
Euser, S. (2016). The prevalence of child sexual abuse in out-of-home care: increased risk for children with a mild intellectual disability. *Journal of Applied Research in Intellectual Disabilities, 29*: 83–92.

Fonagy, P. (2003). Towards a developmental understanding of violence. *British Journal of Psychiatry, 183*: 190–192.

Frankish, P. (2016). *Disability Psychotherapy: An Innovative Approach to Trauma-Informed Care.* London: Karnac.

Freud, S. (1905d). *Three Essays on the Theory of Sexuality. S. E., 7.* London: Hogarth.

Great Britain Equality and Human Rights Commission (2011). *Hidden in Plain Sight: Inquiry into Disability-Related Harassment. Executive Summary.* http://www.equalityhumanrights.com/en

Holland, K. (2011). Factsheet: learning disabilities. *British Institute of Learning Disabilities*, Birmingham.

McCabe, M. P. (1993). Sex education programs for people with mental retardation. *Mental Retardation, 31*: 377–387.

Mitra, M., Mouradian, V. E., & Diamond, M. (2011). Sexual violence and victimization against men with disabilities. *American Journal of Preventative Medicine, 41*: 494–497.

Morgan, D., & Ruszczynski, S. (2007). *Lectures on Violence, Perversion, and Delinquency.* London: Karnac.

O'Driscoll, D. (2009). Psychotherapy and intellectual disability: a historical view. In: T. Cottis (Ed.), *Intellectual Disability, Trauma and Psychotherapy* (pp. 20–44). London: Routledge.

Reitter, S., Bryen, D. N., & Shachar, I. (2007). Adolescents with intellectual disabilities as victims of abuse. *Journal of Intellectual Disabilities, 11*: 371–387.

Sinason, V. (1992). *Mental Handicap and the Human Condition: New Approaches from the Tavistock.* London: Free Association Books.

Spencer, N. (2005). Disabling conditions and registration for child abuse and neglect: a population-based study. *Pediatrics, 116*: 609–613.

Stoller, R. J. (1976). *Perversion: The Erotic Form of Hatred.* Hassocks: Harvester Press.

Symington, N. (1992). Countertransference with mentally handicapped clients. In: A. Waitman & S. Conboy-Hill (Eds.), *Psychotherapy and Mental Handicap* (pp. 132–138). London: Sage.

Welldon, E. V. (1988). *Mother, Madonna, Whore: The Idealization and Denigration of Motherhood.* London: Free Association Books.

Welldon, E. V. (2011). *Playing with Dynamite: A Personal Approach to the Psychoanalytic Understanding of Perversions, Violence and Criminality.* London: Karnac.

Wolfensberger, W. (1987). *The New Genocide of Handicapped and Afflicted People.* Syracuse: New York.

CHAPTER SIX

Sexual cruelty in the marital bed: unconscious sadism in non-forensic couples*

Brett Kahr

When wedding dresses catch on fire

Back in the late tenth century, more than one thousand years ago, an aristocrat called Foulques Nerra—sometimes known as "Fulk the Black"—reigned over the *comté* of Anjou in the heart of France. A devout Christian who had founded numerous abbeys and monasteries, and a patron of architecture who had built many castles, Foulques Nerra had also established a school for the education of the poor. But like many medieval potentates, Foulques dedicated himself not only to charitable works but, also, to violence; and over many years, he distinguished himself in bloody combat, defeating the forces of Conan, the duc de Bretagne, in the Battle of Conquereuil in 992, killing his enemy's son, Alain.

Foulques Nerra did not, however, confine his murderousness to the battlefield. It seems that he also practised early medieval siege warfare at home. In the year 999, Foulques had discovered his countess, Élisabeth de Vendôme, *in flagrante* with a goatherd and, desperate for retribution, the nobleman had his wife bedecked in her wedding dress and

---

then burned alive in the marketplace of Angers, the capital of Anjou (Guillot, 1972; Seward, 2014; cf. de Salies, 1874), in an act described by one medieval source as an *"horribili incendio combusta"* (quoted in Guillot, 1972, p. 25, fn. 129).

It seems uncertain that the fervent French Catholics of the tenth century regarded the vicious, unspeakable immolation of the approximately twenty-year-old *comtesse* Élisabeth as an act of domestic violence. Steeped in a climate of spousal abuse and frequent executions, these medieval Angevins might well have conceptualised the burning as justifiable punishment for the countess's adulterous sin. But from our twenty-first-century perspective, it would be impossible to regard this act of brutality as anything other than the most vicious of marital attacks. By setting fire to his wife—a crime that would today land a man in Broadmoor Hospital for the criminally insane—and by having insisted that Élisabeth, little more than a late adolescent, should be burned in the very gown that she had worn on the day of their wedding, Foulques Nerra has become immortalised as one of the most gruesome perpetrators of marital sadism in history.

Although we cannot excuse the murderousness of Foulques for sanctioning this uxoricide, let us not forget that the Angevin count had done so because of his *wife's* infidelity with a farmhand. This tale from medieval French history serves as a vicious reminder that in many, if not in all, cases of marital explosion, each member of the couple might have contributed in some way or ways to the final outcome.

One could of course cite numerous other instances of sexual cruelty between spouses throughout the centuries. In fact, one need not search very far for evidence (e.g., Bloch, 1991; Bourke, 2007; Butler, 2007; Goldberg, 2008).

Consider, for instance, one of the cruellest forms of sexual sadism in marriage, namely, rape. Indeed, for many centuries, men could, and did, readily force themselves sexually upon their spouses, claiming that the mere act of marriage constituted a woman's consent to intercourse in the first place. The eminent American sociologist and traumatologist Professor David Finkelhor studied spousal rape in Boston, Massachusetts; and in a landmark study, he and his colleague Dr Kersti Yllo discovered that rape occurred in approximately three per cent of these American marriages, and further, that one would be much more likely to be raped by a formally married spouse or a cohabiting partner than by a stranger (Finkelhor & Yllo, 1985). Extrapolating this data to a British sample, one could estimate that, based on Finklehor's and Yllo's findings, approximately six hundred thousand British women have suffered formal rape at the hands of their husbands; while countless others have had to endure unwanted sexual contact of various types. Fortunately, although many countries worldwide have, in recent years, declared spousal rape illegal, including, of course, Great Britain, many others have not; and at the present time, no fewer than thirty-eight countries, including Afghanistan, Bahrain, Ethiopia, Haiti, Iran, Laos, Libya, Morocco, Saudi Arabia, Syria, Uganda, and Zambia, do not prosecute men for raping their wives or for committing other acts of sexual sadism upon their wedded partners.

Gross sexual violence occurs far too frequently within the context of long-term marital relationships, and always with disastrous consequences, including the infliction of physical and psychological damage. Fortunately, most married couples never engage in such clinically sadistic behaviours. Indeed, the vast majority of intimate partners treat one another's physical bodies with a reasonable degree of respect, and refrain from the use of sexual force.

But one need not be a violent, acting-out forensic patient—a rapist or a torturer, for instance—to perpetrate deep cruelty upon one's spousal partner. Often, some of the "nicest" people—including those from privileged, well-bred, well-spoken, and well-educated families—will treat their intimates with shocking viciousness, either physical or verbal, during sexual encounters. Many people, in fact, will reserve their most primitive and aggressive urges *specifically*, if not *exclusively*, for their long-term marital partners. And often, in consequence, the bedroom will become a boxing ring in which otherwise normal-neurotic couples might come to concretise some of their most sadistic tendencies.

Although I began my mental health career working in the forensic field with murderers, paedophiles, arsonists, rapists, and others who had committed acts of shocking abuse, I have accumulated far more experience in recent decades with ordinary, warm-hearted, honourable, philanthropic, and civic-minded people who vote for the Labour Party, who read *The Guardian* newspaper, who make charitable contributions to worthwhile organisations, and who volunteer from time to time at the local soup kitchen *by day*, yet who, nevertheless, will sometimes—indeed often—become deceptive, contemptuous, humiliating, and vengeful towards their spouses *by night*.

Those of us who work in the arena of marital mental health, as couple psychotherapists, couple psychoanalysts, or as couple counsellors, have a unique opportunity to discover the hidden shadows of normal-neurotic marriages at very close range. Indeed, we now understand far more about violence in the ordinary couple than in the forensic couple (cf. Motz, 2014), in large measure because most severe forensic patients live in prisons or hospitals where mental health colleagues have little or no licence or opportunity to work with the spouses.

In view of the increased understanding of violence—especially sexual violence—in non-forensic couples (e.g., Weitzman, 2000), what have we come to learn about the origins of such cruelty, about its function, and also, about its treatment?

In the pages that follow, I shall offer copious clinical vignettes in an effort to sketch a psychodiagnostic terrain of the different types of sexual hurt inflicted by otherwise ordinary, law-abiding citizens. I shall then provide some thoughts about how the psychological clinician can better engage with these stories in work with both individuals and with couples. In all instances, I have, of course, altered the names and other obvious identifying biographical details of the individuals and couples concerned. Otherwise, I have refrained from any distortion of the data that I have heard over the years in my consulting room.

A typology of neurotic sexual cruelty

Violence towards one's spouse manifests itself in many forms, and will often be underpinned by eroticism. Indeed, in the non-forensic population, spousal sexual sadism exists along a continuum, ranging from seemingly minor acts of unkindness and insensitivity in the marital bedroom, characterised by only small amounts of acting-out, to those of a more severe nature, marked by a very considerable degree of acting-out and consequent destruction. Let us now explore the panopticon of the different degrees and varieties of sexual sadism in the marital relationship, which might form the template of a typology of sexual cruelty.

Bodily evacuation as a form of sadism

In the non-forensic sample of individuals and couples that one meets in an out-patient setting—often an independent psychotherapy office—one becomes immediately aware of a vast range of acts of sexual unkindness. At one extreme, I recall the case of "Archibald", a hospital administrator, and "Betty", a nurse—a longstanding married couple with six children—who generally enjoyed one another's company and who had a capacity to make one another laugh. Archibald and Betty presented for couple psychotherapy one year after the death of Betty's mother, a bereavement that had plunged her into a moderate depression. Betty's mother had provided enormous support to the entire family, helping to look after the six children; consequently, her death left Betty deeply heartbroken. Yet in spite of Betty's melancholia, the couple still enjoyed a vigorous sexual life.

One evening, Archibald returned home from the pub, where this hulking man, with broad shoulders, had consumed twelve pints of lager in swift succession. Archibald could generally guzzle as many as eight pints without experiencing any adverse effects, but after twelve of these drinks, he felt more than usually woozy. As he explained, Betty's newfound depressed mood states had caused him distress, and consequently, he treated himself to four additional pints in order to fortify himself against the gloomy atmosphere at home. Later that evening, after the children had gone to sleep, Archibald and Betty went to bed and began to fondle one another, and soon proceeded to engage in coitus.

In the midst of penetration, Archibald began to wretch. Fortunately, he removed himself from inside his wife, and staggered off the bed, and then vomited profusely on the floor, covering Betty's discarded clothes. Although such an encounter between a drunk husband and a depressed wife would be of little interest to a family lawyer—one certainly cannot sue successfully for divorce as the result of a single episode of vomiting—Archibald's behaviour caused Betty great disgust, and for several weeks thereafter, she developed a phobic anxiety that her husband might actually vomit upon her. In view of Betty's depression, she had *already* begun to feel disgusted and dirty. And thus, when her husband discharged himself in the middle of sexual intercourse, Betty felt that the external world of vomitus both confirmed and exacerbated what she had already begun to experience in her internal world, soiled by death and by consequent bereavement.

When Betty disclosed this information in a couple psychotherapy session, Archibald—usually quite compassionate—told Betty brusquely, "Oh, for fuck's sake, woman. Get over yourself. I had a few too many drinks. I didn't slap you." This reaction served only to inflame Betty's deep unhappiness in the face of such an unpleasant sexual encounter with her husband, and she then burst into tears. It took a great deal of time as well as much slow, painstaking psychotherapeutic work to help Archibald come to understand the way in which he had felt burdened and resentful about his wife's depression, which had made him feel impotent and useless, and that by drinking so copiously and then vomiting soon thereafter, he had concretised his rage by spewing vomit from his mouth, rather than angry words.

"Cressida" and "Dexter", another normal-neurotic couple, had recently celebrated their silver wedding anniversary. During their first consultation for couple psychotherapy, Dexter, a professional athlete, admitted that he and Cressida, an unemployed artist, had begun to fight "a bit" during recent months, and that their general medical practitioner had recommended "talking therapy". Although Dexter explained that he had agreed to attend for sessions, he had his doubts about psychotherapy, as he believed that he and his wife only had "one little problem". In order to prove to me that he and Cressida had, essentially, a truly great marriage, Dexter then boasted that he and Cressida "make love" every single night, and that consequently, they enjoy a highly satisfying sexual life. During Dexter's introductory speech, Cressida became increasingly ashen and began to fume. After Dexter paused, I turned in her direction, whereupon she exploded. "A great sex life?" she cried. "You think we have a great sex life?" Dexter then began to stumble over his words, uncertain of how to reply.

At this point, Cressida exploded fully and explained to me that, in reality, they do not "make love", and have, in fact, never made love— quite the contrary. She then elaborated that every night Dexter will take Cressida into the bedroom, undress himself fully, and sit astride her naked torso, then masturbate furiously and ejaculate onto her face. By this point, he will have exhausted himself so much, that he will generally fall onto the bed and then succumb to deep sleep until the morning. After narrating an account of this nightly scenario, Cressida burst into tears.

Dexter, an often-charming man who had many friends and who often donated large sums of money to those in need, had absolutely no capacity to express any comfort, tenderness, or regret to Cressida as she cried and screamed in the consulting room. Instead, he explained that he simply cannot stop himself ejaculating so quickly because he finds her so irresistibly beautiful and that he could never imagine being with any other woman. Although Dexter may have intended this as a great compliment, Cressida became even more enraged at this point, and shouted, "Yes, but why do you have to do it on my face? You make me feel so cheap. So disgusting. And you never bring *me* to orgasm. You're so selfish. So cruel!"

One need not be a mental health professional to wonder why Dexter restricted his sexual activities to climaxing upon his wife's face, and why Cressida—ostensibly horrified by this—had endured such a nightly ritual over many long years. What, then, permitted such a complex marito-sexual dynamic to persevere? It might be tempting to describe the couple's nighttime ritual as a type of sadomasochism, character-ised by Dexter's sadistic ejaculation upon his beautiful wife, and by Cressida's masochistic enjoyment for participating in this situation. But as I came to understand the unconscious life of the couple more fully, I came to realise that sadomasochism does not quite accurately describe the situation.

Dexter grew up in the East End of London as the seventh child of very impoverished parents who lived in a tiny two-bedroom flat on a council estate. Dexter described the estate as "disgusting" and "dirty", but boasted that his mother prided herself on cleanliness, and that she had managed to create a completely spotless home in spite of the family's impoverishment and grubby surroundings. The mother never allowed Dexter and his siblings to play outside for fear that they might muddy their clothing. And in spite of having little money for the water bill, each child had to bathe every single day. Dexter's mother, clearly an obsessional woman, also refused to allow her children to walk bare-foot on the beach, on rare family holidays to the seaside, in case one of them might step on something "nasty". Chuckling affectionately, Dexter explained, "My mother was such a fierce lady that any germs would have been far too frightened to enter the front door".

Cressida had a rather more complicated childhood, characterised by a neglectful, alcoholic mother, and by a father who treated her with a cer-tain amount of sexual lasciviousness. Although Cressida's father never laid a hand upon her, she recalled that he took an inordinate amount of interest in the size of her growing breasts, and upon the length of her skirts, making daily comments about her physicality, which she found intrusive and infuriating.

As our work progressed, the couple confessed to me that each night, prior to their sexual ritual, they would drink a bottle of very fine wine at dinner, and then, they would retire to the sitting room and snort some cocaine. This revelation helped me to understand more fully the way in which such complex nightly sexual choreography could be performed again and again.

Dexter and Cressida had never had children, and claimed that they had never wished to do so. In view of the frequent facial ejaculations, I wondered whether the couple had *ever* engaged in traditional coitus, and I enquired about this. Dexter replied that he and Cressida had attempted "old-fashioned" intercourse a few times, but that neither of them had really enjoyed it very much, and that he had a much more powerful orgasm by masturbating himself.

As our psychotherapeutic work proceeded, and as our shared understanding grew, I became increasingly able to speak quite frankly with this couple. Cressida presented the marital dynamic as a veritable crime scene in which Dexter, the perpetrator, committed a foul act upon her body, and that she, Cressida, had no part to play in this abusive situation whatsoever. Dexter, by contrast, considered himself to be a truly worshipful lover, and would defend himself by explaining that most of his male friends had mistresses, or visited prostitutes, or watched pornography, but that he never cheated on his wife, and that he still found her so very exciting.

I offered a rather different conceptualisation, which I shared with the couple in slow, methodical stages.

I hypothesised that the nightly ritual of Dexter masturbating upon Cressida had begun not in the bedroom, but in the dining room, when each kept filling the other's glass with more "fine wine", and then became fuelled further in the sitting room while each of them inhaled cocaine. I compared this routine to that of an athlete warming up before a sporting event, or that of an actor vocalising prior to stepping out on stage. By underscoring this portion of the scenario, I began to explore with Dexter and Cressida whether, in fact, each of them might be more equally complicitous in the staging of the sexual scenario that would follow. At first, Cressida refused to consider that she had any active role in this situation, but eventually, as her defences began to loosen, both she and Dexter could begin to appreciate more fully the way in which they had conspired *as a couple* to script such an evening routine *jointly*.

Integrating our growing knowledge of the biographies of both Dexter and Cressida, we then began to consider the ways in which their highly institutionalised nightly sexual ritual might represent not a creative engagement of lovemaking but, rather, an instance of what Sigmund Freud (1914, p. 490) had first identified as a *Wiederholungszwang*—a "repetition compulsion"—in which people re-stage early childhood experiences relentlessly, without any conscious awareness of doing so.

As our sessions progressed over a period of many months, the couple came to understand more fully that Dexter had suffered from a lifelong obsessional neurosis which he had kept secret from Cressida, and often, from himself. It soon transpired that he had internalised so many of his mother's injunctions about germs and filth that he had developed the habit of washing his hands twenty or thirty times per day, and always furtively so. Whenever he touched his genitals, he would skulk away to the bathroom afterwards, ostensibly in order to urinate but, in fact, he would scrub his organ several times with carbolic soap. Essentially, he found sexual activity particularly dirty, both physically and mentally, and it proved both shaming and relieving for Dexter to verbalise this secret to me and to his wife at long last. Eventually, he plucked up the courage to inform us that he preferred to ejaculate on Cressida's face rather than to insert his penis inside her vagina, as he regarded the female genitalia as particularly unclean. Naturally, such a confession hurt Cressida deeply, and she began to cry, but gradually came to realise that Dexter's revelation did not surprise her in the least. In many ways, she had already known this about her husband and had already sensed his disgust of bodies in general.

I interpreted that Dexter's struggle to penetrate his wife vaginally stemmed in part, perhaps, from his fear of maternal disapproval and from a fear of contamination, but also served as an expression of his hateful feelings towards women generally, starting with his mother who controlled his mind and body so relentlessly, and ending with his wife, onto whom he transferred these powerful affects. Drawing upon the originary observations of Dr Karl Abraham (1917), one of Freud's earliest disciples, I tried to help the couple to understand that the act of ejaculation upon the woman's body might well represent an expression of deep admiration and excitement, but might also constitute a form of angry soiling.

Cressida, too, eventually came to acquire a more sophisticated knowledge of her own role in facilitating what seemed to be, on the surface, an exclusively sadistic sexual interaction, with Dexter as the ejaculating perpetrator and herself as the passive victim. In fact, by drinking wine and using cocaine each night—the necessary preparation for the sexual ritual—Cressida had assisted Dexter in setting the stage for this particular form of erotic theatre, recreating her own role as the passive victim of her father's lecherous and humiliating attentions during her child-hood. But this time, Cressida allowed her husband to ejaculate upon her face, both repeating something unpleasant, but also, then allowing herself to attack Dexter afterwards, constantly insulting him, complaining about him, and humiliating him—something she could never do with her more terrifying father.

Thus, the case of Dexter and Cressida allows us to consider the possibility that the roots of an uncomfortable sexual scenario, laced with hatred, stem from early antecedents, and then become re-enacted inexorably, and without conscious understanding. In this instance, both members of the couple used the marital bed as a laboratory for discharging, evacuating, and projecting early discomfort and disgust into the other: Dexter did so through ejaculation, and Cressida did so by permitting Dexter to treat her as a dustbin, so that she could then avenge herself upon him with cruel verbal taunts.

Regrettably, I cannot elaborate upon the more detailed development of insight in this couple over the course of time, but fortunately, towards the end of treatment, some three years later, Cressida and Dexter had begun to foster a much more loving, much more tender, and much less sadistic style of lovemaking, as well as a much less alcohol-dependent, drug-dependent style of interrelating more generally. Neither member of the couple found our psychotherapeutic work particularly easy or enjoyable; and often, each would take pot shots at me for "subjecting" them to such an arduous process, which I interpreted as a further expression of their wish to evacuate wounded and hateful feelings into the nearest object to hand.

In the two aforementioned vignettes, that of Archibald and Betty—the couple who turned the bedroom into a *vomitorium*—and that of Cressida and Dexter—the couple whose marital chamber became an *ejaculatorium*—each member of the couple participated in equal measure in the creation of the sadistic sexual scenario, using the marital bed as a means of evacuating unpleasant, primitive affects. Although Archibald vomited on Betty's clothing, and Dexter evacuated his semen on Cressida's face, neither couple, to their credit, "acted out" beyond the confines of the marital relationship. Each of these partners managed to preserve their most particularly noxious feelings exclusively for one another, and did so at the same time, and in the same room. In spite of the difficulties, these couples remained very much faithful and intact.

I wish to propose that such instances of evacuation, which remain confined primarily to the bedroom, offer the clinician a great sense of hope. Prognostically, such couples manage treatment reasonably well, if not very well indeed, and will usually remain committed to their marriage. In my experience, such couples rarely divorce or experience what I have come to refer to as a "conjugal aneurysm" (Kahr, 2014).

But sexual sadism can become much more complex, and once the enactments of aggressivity begin to emerge outside of the physical bedroom itself, couples will often experience infinitely more distress. Archibald and Betty, and Cressida and Dexter remained deeply committed to one another. In more advanced cases of marital infidelity—either psychical or physical in nature, and often both—extra-maritality becomes the hallmark of cruelty.

The intra-marital affair and the extra-marital affair

"Elfriede" entered individual psychoanalytical treatment in order to overcome a longstanding inhibition in her professional work. An artist of considerable accomplishment, Elfriede had begun to "freeze" while in her studio, and for several years, she could produce no work at all. Elfriede, married to her childhood sweetheart "Francis", an ophthalmologist, often smirked with a considerable amount of contempt, and would joke that she had married the only blind eye doctor in the United Kingdom, because Francis did not have a clue about his wife.

Indeed, Elfriede led a double life. She spent hours at her computer masturbating to Internet pornography, looking at cyber photographs of handsome men. She also frequented clubs and pubs, wearing tight skirts with no underwear beneath, in the hope that some man would notice her and whisk her away, *Madame Bovary*-style, from her bourgeois life as a doctor's wife. As Francis worked incredibly long hours, Elfriede felt extremely abandoned, in spite of the fact that she enjoyed the financial security afforded by her husband's profession.

Often gripped by strong denial, Elfriede spent a great deal of her session time boasting that Francis had not the slightest inkling about her computer activities or about her many visits to bars; and though she felt triumphant that she could "cheat" on her husband in this way, she also felt extremely desolate that her "blind" ophthalmologist could not see the extent of her unhappiness. Interestingly, although Elfriede devoted much time to the Internet and to her erotic forays into the West

End of London, she never actually succeeded in sleeping with another man. Although various gentlemen bought her drinks and made passes at her, something always stopped her from taking them to bed. Technically, she remained faithful to Francis, but in her private mind she had committed a multitude of infidelities, exemplifying what I have come to refer to as the "intra-marital affair" (Kahr, 2007, p. 32), as opposed to the more familiar extra-marital variety.

The intra-marital affair—a liaison that unfolds predominantly in the mind—may not leave lipstick stains on the collar or hotel receipts in one's handbag or trouser pockets, but this type of internal enactment can cause great psychological devastation nonetheless. Intra-marital affairs—these extraordinarily private and deeply consuming sexual fantasy constellations—serve a multiplicity of functions. In my earlier study of the traumatic origins of the sexual fantasy, I identified as many as fifteen possible conscious and unconscious functions of the sexual fantasy or intra-marital affair, including, *inter alia*, that of an unconscious attack on both oneself and upon one's partner (Kahr, 2007, 2008).

Although sexual fantasies may often serve as great sources of private fun and pleasure, and can often, in the context of a healthy marriage, become an additional reservoir of sexual creativity, such intra-marital affairs serve, for the most part, as uncomfortable refuges which help alienate each spouse from the other. In more extreme cases, especially in those individuals with a pronounced history of emotional and physical trauma, intra-marital affairs become ossified as "erotic tumours" of the mind, which come to dominate all aspects of psychic functioning in much the way that a brain tumour will destroy aspects of healthy cognition. When these erotic tumours erupt, they will often result in what I have earlier identified as the "conjugal aneurysm" (Kahr, 2014).

I cannot, on this occasion, provide a more detailed study of either the aetiology or treatment of Elfriede's intra-marital affair, but I can confirm that she did, indeed, suffer profoundly, and her private sexual preoccupations, which she had never articulated to anyone prior to the start of her psychoanalytical sessions with me, prevented her from enjoying either her professional work as an artist or her marital relationship with a somewhat emotionally unsophisticated but otherwise loyal and decent husband. Elfriede's intra-marital affairs—an expression of sexual sadism towards Francis—bedevilled her mind, but fortunately, an immersion in a lengthy period of intensive, multi-frequency psychoanalytical work helped to contain and to work through the force of her intra-marital preoccupations, and prevent them from becoming ossified as an erotic tumour or from exploding as a conjugal aneurysm.

To her great credit, Elfriede had come to seek help before the volcanic destruction of her marriage; and having undergone protracted psychoanalytical treatment, her spousal relationship remains intact and enriched to this day. But other individuals and couples who suffer from the psychopathologies of sexual fantasy will often arrive at our consulting rooms only *after* the conjugal aneurysm has erupted with devastating consequences.

"Gwilym", a successful barrister, devoted his life to public service, and had, as a result of his hard labours, developed a fine reputation in his field of legal expertise. He often lavished his wife "Hester" with expensive pieces of jewellery, and he always made a point of protecting his family diary so that he would never do any paperwork at weekends; instead, he spent every Saturday morning playing football with his son, and every Saturday afternoon accompanying his daughter to ballet classes. He devoted Sunday mornings to cooking an enormous roast meal which he and his wife and children enjoyed greatly; and later in the day, Gwilym would supervise the pleasant ritual of watching a family-friendly film with his loved ones. On paper, he had the perfect life.

But every night, after Hester went to bed, Gwilym would sneak downstairs into his study, lock the door, and masturbate to a particular genre of Internet pornography. Although he identified himself as "one hundred per cent heterosexual", he had become quite obsessed with pre-operative transsexuals, and would climax to visual images of men with penises as well as newly developed, hormonally induced breasts, bedecked in lacy lingerie. These Internet sessions caused Gwilym a great deal of shame, but they also provided him with a degree of unrivalled sexual excitement which eclipsed any pleasure that he had experienced with his otherwise beautiful and loving wife Hester.

As one might imagine, those who perform sexual activities outside of the bedroom will wish to conceal their infidelities—even those of a "virtual" cyber nature—but, at the same time, many will also harbour an unconscious wish to be discovered, in the secret hope that by doing so, a marital crisis may be provoked and then, ultimately, treated. And so, in spite of many years of creeping quietly into his study, Hester had eventually come to notice her husband's late-night disappearances; and on one fateful evening, when Gwilym had failed to lock the door to his study, she burst in on him unannounced, and found him engaged in a live "cyber-chat" with a male-to-female pre-operative transsexual.

At this moment, Hester's world collapsed entirely, and she not only screamed at Gwilym for his tremendous duplicitousness and "perversion", she also screamed at herself for her naiveté, recognising that she could no longer respect or believe the very special, beloved man in whom she had placed every ounce of her trust. At Hester's insistence, she and Gwilym then arranged a consultation to see me for marital psychotherapy.

Gwilym never actually met a transsexual man in person. He never exchanged bodily fluids with anyone other than his wife. But his copious cyber activities, indicative of a strong set of intra-marital affairs and erotic tumours, provoked a conjugal aneurysm of great proportions which made Hester feel that she had lived a lie throughout her entire marriage. I must confess that upon hearing of this aneurytic marriage, I had initially assumed—quite wrongly, I must confess—that such spousal turmoil could never be survived, and that Hester and Gwilym had come to see me in order to find a more human way of divorcing.

But the couple loved each other greatly, and after five years of psychotherapy, had managed to come to experience understanding and even forgiveness. Once again, I cannot discuss the complexities of the treatment itself in the context of such a brief communication, but I can report that through our work, Gwilym came to conceptualise his need for a fantasied sexual experience with a male-female person as the result of much early deprivation from both his mother and his father. And Hester not only developed a greater, more sensitive appreciation of Gwilym's complicated sexual mind but also came to realise the ways in which her own infantile rage, never before contained or treated, had helped to provoke Gwilym to seek a Hester-free refuge in his study late at night.

The cases of Elfriede and Francis, and of Gwilym and Hester, typify the widespread nature of what we might come to consider as "disorders of sexual fantasy" in otherwise healthy, law-abiding, and compassionate individuals. Neither Elfriede nor Gwilym had ever perpetrated acts of discernible cruelty against their children, their friends, their colleagues, or other members of society. Instead, they reserved their private sadistic attacks for their spouses, and ultimately, in view of the consequences, for themselves.

Elfriede and Gwilym—the two fantasists under consideration—differ from Archibald, who vomited on his wife, and from Dexter, who ejaculated on his spouse, because the former individuals, Elfriede and Gwilym, "acted out" *beyond* the space of the marital bedroom *behind* their partners' backs, while the latter, Archibald and Dexter, did so in the *presence* of their wives. Of course, I do not wish to propose so crude a theory as to suggest that those who perpetrate sadistic acts in front of their partners may be less dangerous than those who do so more secretively. The very reality of marital rape would contradict such an assertion completely. But I do wish to suggest that when the sadistic enactment occurs in full view of the partner, then the cry for help becomes more apparent more quickly, and each member of the marital pair has a greater opportunity for awareness and for seeking psychological treatment.[1]

Sadistic enactments as a defence against death

Sexual insensitivity, sexual thoughtlessness, sexual narcissism, and sexual cruelty can cause a great deal of distress to partners. Thus far, we have examined what might transpire when partners treat one another's bodies or bodily space with unkindness, or when spouses "cheat" on each other in a fantasmatic way, often assisted by the Internet. But what happens when infidelity moves beyond the realms of fantasy and into the arena of bodily enactments with another living person outside of the marital home?

For the non-forensic couple—those who never commit arrestable crimes such as rape or murder or domestic violence—sadistic infidelity may well be the most serious expression of cruelty, and it presents far greater challenges to both the couple and to the clinician. "Isaac" had just turned forty. A successful banker with lots of money to spare, this man travelled extensively for work, and during his many trips abroad, he spent many evenings alone in luxury hotels. Separated from his wife "Jessica" and from his four young children, Isaac often arranged for prostitutes to visit him in his hotel suite and engaged in a variety of sexual activities.

Although Isaac explained that he found most of these prostitutes to be "disposable", one young woman, in particular, a nineteen-year-old called "Katerina", had really captivated him, and he began to meet with her more frequently, often flying abroad just to see her. Before long, Isaac stopped paying Katerina for sex and he eventually established her as a second spouse, and even purchased a beautiful apartment for her. In due course, Katerina became pregnant with twins, and eventually,

Isaac found himself supporting two wives and six children, as well as both a British household and a Continental household.

Isaac's concretely enacted infidelity can be traced to a multitude of sources. But above all, we must note that this series of visits to prostitutes and the creation of a second marriage to Katerina all occurred in the wake of his fortieth birthday. During the course of one-to-one psychotherapy with this man, it did not surprise me to learn that Isaac's father had also had a conjugal aneurysm at the age of forty and had left Isaac's mother in a most traumatic way. He simply disappeared, abandoning both wife and son forever. The ten-year-old Isaac never saw his father again.

To Isaac's credit, perhaps, he continued to maintain very regular contact—physical, emotional, as well as financial—with his wife Jessica and with his four British children. He never abandoned them in the completely callous way his own father had done. Although Isaac had repeated a parental, intergenerational trauma, he had minimised the extent of the abandonment. But in spite of the fact that he did not disappear on Jessica and his children in the way his father had disappeared on him, Isaac nonetheless committed an act of great infidelity—a form of sexual sadism—which cost him dearly. Not only did he find himself crippled by the cost of maintaining his two wives, six children, and two household establishments, he also found himself virtually bankrupt after Jessica discovered his "double life" and sued for divorce, winning an impressive settlement which cost Isaac millions.

As a man who had only recently entered his fifth decade of life, Isaac began to fear death greatly. Indeed, in the wake of his divorce, he found it extremely difficult to differentiate between the emotional death that he experienced when Jessica took the children and left him from his own sense of having an ageing body. In our psychological work together, we gradually came to appreciate the way in which Isaac's attraction to prostitutes and, in particular, to the youthful Continental Katerina, served as a means of eroticisation as a defence against deadliness—a common form of "acting out" in the middle years of life in which one replaces death with sex in the hope that the birth of a new baby will minimise the pain and the work required from each of us at facing the severe limitation of time.

Throughout psychotherapy, Isaac struggled to appreciate the full extent of the way in which his deep infidelity and his creation of a second family with Katerina had caused immense pain to his wife Jessica and to his four children. During many sessions, Isaac referred to Jessica as a "fucking bitch" for having hired such a "shark" of a lawyer who kept asking for more and more money in the divorce settlement. Isaac experienced great difficulty appreciating his deep, sadistic betrayal of Jessica. If he had allowed himself greater sensitivity, he might never have committed such a series of enactments in the first place.

I shall conclude this portion of the chapter with one further clinical vignette, which illustrates most shockingly the true depth and the profound viciousness of sexual sadism in spousal relationships. "Lester", a businessman, and "Martina", a schoolteacher, had married during their early thirties and had remained in a very long marriage of more than twenty-five years; but throughout their time together, Lester had cheated on innumerable occasions. The couple arrived at my office in a dreadful state because one year previously, Martina had received a diagnosis of lymphoma, and had subsequently undergone several rounds of debilitating chemotherapy and radiotherapy which caused her to lose all of her hair, and which produced great nausea and fatigue. Owing to the gravity of her cancer, Martina had hoped that Lester would cease his infidelities and become a good caretaker; and indeed, he did promise that he would look after her throughout this dreadful medical ordeal.

Tragically, Lester perpetrated one of the greatest acts of marital sadism that I have encountered in over thirty-five years of clinical practice. It seems that after Lester dropped Martina off at hospital for her chemotherapy sessions, he would then, quite frequently, check into a hotel room round the corner from the hospital, and have sex with Martina's younger and healthier sister, whom he had always fancied. A skilled philanderer, Lester had managed to keep the details of these furtive encounters secret from Martina, but her sister "Norma", riddled with guilt, confessed what had happened in order to clear her troubled conscience. To her great credit, Martina refrained from killing herself in desperation, and also from injuring her husband and her sister, which many other women might have done in such comparable, horrific circumstances.

I could expound at great length on the psychodynamic aspects of this case, and upon the role of the childhood histories of both Lester and Martina, and also of her sister Norma, in creating such an unholy triangle. But in this context, I have chosen to undertake the more primary task of describing a typology of sadism; and no discussion of the topic would be complete without providing an indication of the magnitude of cruelty in otherwise normal-neurotic marriages between essentially law-abiding, decent citizens. I can report with heavy heart that in the midst of our efforts to unravel and treat this exceptionally painful conjugal explosion, Martina succumbed to her lymphoma, and she died at the age of fifty-six years.

The case of the forty-year-old Isaac, volcanically immersed in a profound mid-life crisis, which prompted him to find a second wife and to create a second family; and the case of Lester, a long-term marital despoiler, who slept with his wife's sister during chemotherapy sessions, underscore the painful association between sexual infidelity, marital sadism, and the struggle with death anxiety. In each instance, one member of the couple endeavoured in quite a primitive manner to defend against the inevitability of ageing and death by introducing eroticism into the mixture, in the vain hope that by suddenly becoming sexual, one could deny the reality of an ailing body.[2]

Torching the marital bedroom

In 2007, I published the results of a five-year study, the British Sexual Fantasy Research Project, which surveyed and analysed the sexual behaviours and, in particular, the erotic fantasies of a randomised sample of some 13,553 adult Britons (Kahr, 2007), supplemented by comparable data on some 3,617 American adults, published the following year (Kahr, 2008). The study of British sexuality revealed that as many as thirty-six per cent of adults, aged eighteen or older, have kissed someone other than a regular spouse or partner, outside of the relationship; twenty-five per cent have fondled someone other than a spouse or partner; eighteen per cent have engaged in extra-marital oral sex; twenty-four per cent in extra-marital vaginal sex; and five per cent in extra-marital anal sex (Kahr, 2007). In each of these instances, men in partnerships indulged themselves more frequently than women ... but not much more. For instance, although twenty-eight per cent of partnered males boasted one or more experiences of extra-marital vaginal sex, as many as twenty per cent of partnered females did so as well. Translated from percentages into actual figures, this indicates that approximately 11,000,000 British adults have submitted themselves to extra-marital vaginal penetration.

When we examine sexual fantasies, as opposed to sexual behaviours, the incidence becomes infinitely greater; and hardly a man or woman alive will not have climaxed to the thought of sexual congress with someone other than his or her long-term partner. This should not surprise us, as the indulgence in sexual fantasy has for many centuries helped to protect us from actual, forensic infidelities. If we take a pretty co-worker or a handsome stranger to bed *in our minds*, we might, perhaps, be less likely to do so in the "outside" world.

But when one explores the content of many of these sexual fantasies, one finds that the average Briton often achieves climax by masturbating about extra-marital sex, with as many as forty-one per cent of British adults having admitted to the erotic fantasy of sexual relations with someone else's partner. Furthermore, as many as twenty-nine per cent of the adult British sample have reported having had fantasies of being dominant or aggressive during sexual activity, and thirty-three per cent having had comparable fantasies of being submissive or passive during sexual activity, with as many as thirteen per cent enjoying spanking someone else, and twelve per cent fantasising about being spanked. As many as twenty-three per cent of adults reported sexual pleasure at the thought of tying up someone else, and twenty-five per cent of adults reported sexual pleasure at the prospect of being tied up (Kahr, 2007). Clearly, the inter-relationship between sexuality, aggression, and infidelity remains extremely intimate.

In the preceding pages, I have endeavoured to outline a typology of sexual sadism in the non-forensic couple, those partners who constitute the vast majority of the world's population. None of the members of the couples described herein have ever set their spouses on fire as Foulques Nerra, the medieval Angevin *comte*, had done back in the tenth century. Indeed, none of the couples in my clinical survey have ever, to the best of my knowledge, received even so much as a parking ticket from the local traffic warden. All of the men and women with whom I have worked have led reasonably exemplary lives, have paid their taxes, and have helped old men and women cross the road. They have, indeed, proved to be model citizens except, perhaps, in the bedroom.

And whether by vomiting on each other, by ejaculating on each other, by masturbating to Internet pornography throughout the small hours of the night, by keeping a second home, a second wife, and a second child in another country, or by sleeping with the sibling of one's spouse while that spouse undergoes chemotherapy, all of the aforementioned couples have found a way of expressing sadism, thus soiling the potentialities of the marital bedroom. In most cases, one partner holds the distinction of being the overt instigator of the cruelty. For example, in the case of Gwilym, the man who spent hours engaged in Internet cyber chats with pre-operative transsexuals, any court of law would describe him as the perpetrator, and his wife Hester as the innocent victim. After all, *she* had never masturbated with a stranger over the Internet. Only Gwilym had done so. Of course, *in sensu stricto*, only Gwilym had committed an act of infidelity, but those of us who work from a couple psychoanalytical perspective have come to realise that even though one partner engages in the forensic enactment of infidelity, both partners in a marriage will have contributed to the creation of the unconscious emotional climate in which such enactments become possible, even necessary, in order to maintain psychological equilibrium, and in order to protect the couple from even worse marital violence. When, during couple psychotherapy, Hester screamed at Gwilym, she did so with such ferocity that I often wished that I had brought a pair of ear plugs to the consulting room. I realised of course that any wife who discovered her husband *in flagrante* might wish to raise her voice in such a pained and anguished way. But as I came to know this couple better, I learned from Gwilym that Hester had screamed at him night and day, long before he had ever had access to something called the Internet. I can confess to you to the screaming became so persistent, and so penetrative, that on one occasion, a colleague who works in the adjoining consulting room in my office building complained to me afterwards about the noise level. This vignette helped me to realise that although one member of the couple often commits the "crime", *both* members of the couple have facilitated its ultimate staging.

Many people often lambaste Sigmund Freud for having foregrounded the importance of both sexuality and aggression as the dominant features of the human unconscious mind. Whether Freud overestimated the role of such basic drives remains a matter for debate. But as a couple mental health worker, I might even be inclined to suggest that Freud may have *underestimated* the role of destructive sexuality and aggression in the intimate partner relationship, because as a couple worker, I often see evidence of little else.

In the clinical consulting room, we invariably encounter evidence of the painfully close admixture of these two most powerful drives. "Oscar", an elderly man, had developed a severe bronchitis, and he languished for days and days in the marital bed. Once, he asked his wife "Priscilla" to bring him a cup of hot tea to ease his aching throat.

Priscilla returned with the tea … four and a half hours later, claiming that she had forgotten all about her husband's request, and had become engrossed in watching a film. Oscar, too weak to move, could not shout to her for assistance. Even such a seemingly simple example of sadism in the marital bedroom underscores how one need not dress like a dominatrix and whip one's spouse in order to make one's spouse feel quite horribly beaten.

In most instances, such enactments in the bedroom might be described as deeply unconscious, and most of my patients have absolutely no idea why they engage in sexual cruelty in the bedroom. "Quincy", a man with whom I had worked on a one-to-one basis in individual psychoanalysis, spent months and months explaining how much closer he had become to his wife "Rose", and how much better their sexual life had become in recent months. Imagine my surprise, as well as Quincy's surprise, when he told me, one day, that he had recently begun an extra-marital affair with a woman called "Saskia". Curiously, each time Quincy took Saskia—the new girlfriend—to bed, he could not attain an erection; but when he had sex with Rose—the wife—he managed to become completely tumescent. This made no sense to Quincy, and he joked that he would be remembered as "the only man in history who could fuck his wife but not his mistress". Through sustained psychoanalytical work, Quincy and I came to realise that this episode of marital enactment—taking a mistress—had occurred in the wake of his ninth wedding anniversary to Rose; and that this might mirror quite precisely the fact that Quincy's father had begun to live with a mistress shortly after Quincy's ninth birthday. Quincy found the parallel quite striking, and soon came to realise that he had become engulfed in the unconscious re-enactment of an early childhood trauma, without realising that he had done so. A few weeks thereafter, he broke off his affair with Saskia, and resumed his very satisfying sexual relationship with Rose!

Marital unkindness appears in many guises, and on the surface, many acts of thoughtlessness appear to be devoid of a sexual substratum. During my very first consultation with "Thérèse" and "Ugo", a Continental couple, I took a moment to clarify the correct spelling of their names and to write down their home address and telephone numbers. I turned to Thérèse and asked, "Would I be correct that you spell your name with two accents—an acute accent on the first 'e', and a grave accent on the second 'e'?" She confirmed this to be the case, whereupon Ugo exclaimed, "My word, I never knew that you had accents on your name". Thérèse became utterly heartbroken that her husband of five years did not seem to know something as fundamental as the spelling of her name. It then emerged that this couple, in spite of their rows, had sex constantly; and it soon became apparent that their sexual life served primarily as an erotic defence against talking to one another. They managed physicality very well, but they could not relate in any other way, not least in terms of basic literacy, emotional or otherwise.

Sometimes, the unkindness between couples may not seem unkind at all. "Vincent", a young college student, got drunk at a party, and took "Wendy", another drunk student, to bed. In his session, he boasted to me that as Wendy had had too much to drink, he thought it best not to penetrate her, in case she might regret this in the morning. Vincent thus presented himself as a true gentleman. But as he lay on the couch in my office, free associating, he then immediately became reminded of a newspaper article that he had read some years ago about an American university student—a male—who had entered a sorority house and had shot all of the women dead with a machine gun. Although Vincent had, indeed, behaved in a thoughtful manner by not forcing himself upon a drunken female, his free association revealed that he found himself struggling with sadistic desires nonetheless, unsurprisingly so, in view of their ubiquity in psychological life.

In many respects, we save our most unkind components for the person we claim to love most. We do so, in part, because we can. If we offend the hostess of a dinner party by insulting her food, we know that we will not be invited back again, and thus, we cannot "use" that venue as a vehicle for the discharge of sadism. But if we critique our spouse's food, we know that such an evacuation must be tolerated and will be tolerated; and therefore, we return again and again and continue to perpetrate the same unconscious crime. Sometimes, in more cynical moments, having spent long days in the office working with rageful couples, I do wonder whether we marry our partners primarily as an expression of love, or rather, as an opportunity to express hatred. Such a dynamic epitomises the shrewd observation that Donald Winnicott (1970, p. 262) offered many years ago, namely, that "What is good is always being destroyed", and that we all have a very powerful need to "use" objects as a means of equilibrating our own faulty sense of self (cf. Winnicott, 1969).

In an ideal world, the marital bed should be a place where a couple can experience tenderness, eroticism, bodily safety, and psychological comfort. It could, and should, be a place where partners can find a refuge from the anxieties of the world, or even dream creatively about how they might change the world. It may be a venue in which spouses can read a book, watch a film, welcome young children on a Saturday morning, play with the cat and dog, and, of course, sleep in peace. But owing to the widespread nature of early trauma and the sadism which devolves therefrom, the bedroom often becomes a place of cruelty which can manifest itself in both gross and subtle forms, even among those who have no criminal history in other areas of their lives.

As mental health professionals, we must continue to become more bold, more adept, and more diplomatic at working with couples to help them unearth, and then to articulate, the many ways in which sadism can blight the landscape of an otherwise non-sadistic marital couple. As we know, one need not set one's spouse on fire in order to torch the bedroom. Fortunately, as we become better adept at the art of couple psychoanalysis and couple psychotherapy, we will ultimately, one hopes, prove to be more effective at helping to extinguish these deadly marital flames.

Acknowledgements

I had the privilege of presenting a somewhat shortened version of this chapter as part of the talks on "Working Psychotherapeutically with Sadism: A Seminar Series for Psychotherapists and Psychologists", organised by Confer, in London, on 10 October 2014. I thank my long-standing colleague Ms Jane Ryan for her kind invitation to speak, and for having chaired the meeting so graciously. I also wish to offer my grateful thanks to the members of the audience for their many spirited questions and contributions.

Likewise, I extend my deep appreciation to Dr Amita Sehgal for her considered and intelligent work on the editing of this book. Drawing upon Jane Ryan's initial concept of exploring contemporary psycho-analytical views on sadism, Amita Sehgal has helpfully assembled the chapters herein within a useful developmental framework. I remain grateful to both women for their insights and for their collegiality.

Notes

1. The disorders of sexual fantasy, as I have indicated, often serve as the bedrock of infidelity, either in the form of an intra-marital affair or an extra-marital affair. When I first presented this essay to a group of mental health colleagues, a member of the audience asked whether

I regard all affairs as inherently pathological. This particular individual noted that many couples engage in "swinging" or in "open marriage" and so forth; other audience members noted that the partner of a very ill spouse might sometimes take a lover (e.g., as in the case of an elderly man whose wife suffers from Alzheimer's disease and who might, understandably, have another partner for sexual relationships). One would need a further chapter in order to provide a clearer answer to this question, which concerns both clinicians and ethicists. On this occasion, I cannot offer a fully articulated position about the inherent pathology or non-pathology of the extra-marital affair or the intra-marital affair, for that matter; but I can report that in all the couples who have presented for psychotherapeutic treatment, each affair or instance of infidelity caused great pain and suffering to all the people concerned.

2. In the context of such a relatively brief communication, I have elected to focus predominantly on three particular types of sexual cruelty, namely, the use of bodily evacuations, the intra-marital affair and the extra-marital affair (or the disorders of sexual fantasy), and finally, the use of cruelty as a defence against death anxiety. But couples have an infinite capacity to express marital sadism in other ways. One could, of course, also examine other varieties of potential sexual cruelty, namely, the withholding of sex as a form of aggression (e.g., Friedman, 1962; Grier, 2001), as well as the practice of bondage and dominance (or "consensual kink") as potential forms of sexual cruelty (Ortmann & Sprott, 2013). These complex subjects deserve much further consideration.

References

Abraham, K. (1917). Über Ejaculatio praecox. *Internationale Zeitschrift für ärztliche Psychoanalyse*, 4: 171–186.

Bloch, R. H. (1991). *Medieval Misogyny and the Invention of Western Romantic Love*. Chicago, IL: University of Chicago Press.

Bourke, J. (2007). *Rape: A History from 1860 to the Present Day*. London: Virago.

Butler, S. M. (2007). *The Language of Abuse: Marital Violence in Later Medieval England*. Leiden: Koninklijke Brill.

De Salies, A. (1874). *Histoire de Foulques-Nerra: Comte d'Anjou. D'Après les chartres contemporaines et les anciennes chroniques. Suivie de l'office du Saint-Sépulcre de l'abbaye de Beaulieu dont les leçons forment une chronique inédite. Avec 12 planches et une grande carte*. Paris: J.-B. Dumoulin, Libraire, and Angers: E. Barassé, Imprimerie-Libraire.

Finkelhor, D., & Yllo, K. (1985). *License to Rape: Sexual Abuse of Wives*. New York: Holt, Rinehart and Winston.

Freud, S. (1914). Weitere Ratschläge zur Technik der Psychoanalyse: II. Erinnern, Wiederholen und Durcharbeiten. *Internationale Zeitschrift für ärztliche Psychoanalyse, 2*: 485–491.

Friedman, L. J. (1962). *Virgin Wives: A Study of Unconsummated Marriages*. London: Tavistock, and Springfield, IL: Charles C. Thomas.

Goldberg, J. (2008). *Communal Discord, Child Abduction, and Rape in the Later Middle Ages*. New York: Palgrave Macmillan/St Martin's Press.

Grier, F. (2001). No sex couples, catastrophic change and the primal scene. *British Journal of Psychotherapy, 17*: 474–488.

Guillot, O. (1972). *Le Comte d'Anjou et son entourage au XIe siècle: Tome I. Étude et appendices*. Paris: Éditions A. et J. Picard.

Kahr, B. (2007). *Sex and the Psyche*. London: Allen Lane/Penguin Books.

Kahr, B. (2008). *Who's Been Sleeping in Your Head?: The Secret World of Sexual Fantasies*. New York: Basic Books.

Kahr, B. (2014). The intra-marital affair: from erotic tumour to conjugal aneurysm. Conference on "The Couple in the Room, the Couple in Mind: Reflections from an Attachment Perspective", the Twenty-First John Bowlby Memorial Conference, the Bowlby Centre, Kennedy Lecture Theatre, Wellcome Trust Building, Institute of Child Health, University College London, Holborn, 4 April.

Motz, A. (2014). *Toxic Couples: The Psychology of Domestic Violence*. London: Routledge/Taylor and Francis.

Ortmann, D. M., & Sprott, R. A. (2013). *Sexual Outsiders: Understanding BDSM Sexualities and Communities*. Lanham, MD: Rowman and Littlefield.

Seward, D. (2014). *The Demon's Brood*. London: Constable and Robinson.

Weitzman, S. (2000). *"Not to People Like Us": Hidden Abuse in Upscale Marriages*. New York: Basic Books.

Winnicott, D. W. (1969). The use of an object. *International Journal of Psycho-Analysis, 50*: 711–716.

Winnicott, D. W. (1970). The place of the monarchy. In: D. W. Winnicott, *Home Is Where We Start From: Essays by a Psychoanalyst*, ed. C. Winnicott, R. Shepherd, & M. Davis (pp. 260–268). New York: W. W. Norton, 1986.

CHAPTER SEVEN

Sadism as manifest in the couple relationship

Susan Irving

The aim of this chapter is to present a brief review the psychoanalytic theories of the aetiology of sadism and to extend the application of this understanding to psychotherapeutic work with the couple. I suggest that sadism is primarily an attack upon and defence against, what I will term "the dependent self" and that in couple work this particularly manifests when that attack is exacerbated by pairing with an uncontaining object. I illustrate this with two clinical case examples, one with a couple in which this particular feature of sadism, not entirely obvious in the current literature, emerged during our work together. In the second couple, I believe this phenomenon is equally applicable, albeit with an entirely different presentation. The therapeutic challenges of working with such couples are also considered.

Brief theoretical background

In discussing the death instinct, Freud postulated that an autonomous (non-sexual) aggressive drive is present from the beginning of life and works continually to unbind connections, in contrast to Eros, which works to bind (1920g). Freud distinguished the non-erotic function of the death instinct from sadism. He proposed the notion of a primary masochism, a state in which the death instinct is turned against the self but bound and fused with libido (Freud, 1924c). Masochism then is a power-based defence against the vulnerable self which could otherwise be killed off and rendered inorganic by the death instinct. It is a passive activity. Sadism is an active reversal of masochism; it designates a state of fusion of sexuality with violence against others in order to exercise power over them.

According to the Kleinian view, "early sadistic phantasies are an essential part of normal development and have an important function in the life of the infant. Persecutory anxieites comprise the infant's dread of annihilation by its own destructive impulses, which arise from the death instinct and which are projected as persecutory objects" (Perelberg, 1999, p. 25). However Parens argued that "there is no evidence of destructive or injurious behaviour in children in the absence of experiences of pain, deprivation or suffering … Cruelty and sadism … result from a prolonged failure of the environment to neutralise rage in the infant" (Parens, 1997, pp. 250–266). These differing views form the basis for ongoing debates about the origins of sadism.

In contemporary psychoanalytic discussions, "sadism" is regarded as part of the duality of "sadomasochism", a dynamic fantasy in the mind involving an interaction between the sadistic and the masochistic parts of the personality. When sadism appears prominent, it can be assumed that masochism is present, albeit unconsciously, and vice versa. The term "sadomasochism" is particularly relevant in couple relationships where the two parts can frequently be seen enacted by the two partners.

Generally speaking, the psychoanalytic perspective considers sadomasochistic behaviour involving physical violence as a form of perversion and seriously detrimental to relationships. In perversion, sexual fantasy influences a person's total behaviour (Stoller, 1974). Stoller described perversion as "the erotic form of hatred" arising from "an essential interplay between hostility and sexual desire … [where] anxiety and risk-taking, violence and revenge are hidden in the symptomatology" (1974, p. 432).

De Masi (2003) proposed that sadomasochism is not primarily caused by a deviation from normal sexual development but by "sexualisation of certain drives and instincts causing a distortion of the whole personality" (De Masi, 2003, p. 89). It is as if the psychic energy which is diverted into the perversion causes a distortion to commence, which is then accelerated and confirmed by the rewarding effects of the resultant excitation. This excitation then creates an addictive type of bond which he compares to the addiction to drink or drugs. Central to De Masi's theory is that the relationship to the other is fundamentally destroyed. Indeed, he claims that it is the transgressional destruction of the "other", and also of reality, that heightens the excitement.

Joseph concluded from her work with a man with a perversion, a fetish, that "His perversion affected his relationships with his external and internal objects, as well as his sense of truth and guilt" (1971, p. 449).

These observations have important implications for couple therapy, where it is important to consider the fate of the object in sadomasochistic enactments. De Masi, a psychoanalyst working with adults, refers to his work with individuals and points out that very few sadists present themselves for treatment, because very few consider they have a problem from which they feel they suffer and therefore wish to understand or change.

However, De Masi's conclusions are pertinent to understanding a certain type of sadomasochistic dynamic that couple therapists might observe in the internal worlds of couples: sometimes this dynamic manifests as having an apparently overtly sexual component in the external world, resembling the dramatic acting out of the stereotype of what is now known colloquially as "S and M", but frequently the presentation is entirely different and takes longer to uncover. The common denominator closely resembles what De Masi termed the "sadomasochistic monad", a cell within a complex organism inside which he placed "the mental experience of destructive pleasure" (De Masi, 2003, p. 4). As previously stated, I believe that the degree of destruction of the "other" varies and that, indeed, the presence of some form of "other", maybe merely a part-object, seems essential for the fulfilment of the drama and the success of the enterprise. The survival of a response in the "other" to perpetuate the game also seems necessary.

This distinction parallels two types of violence distinguished by Glasser as the difference between aggression and sadism in terms of the "attitude to the object at the time the act is carried out" (Glasser, 1979, p. 281). In aggression, the aim is to eliminate and destroy the object and the object's fate is irrelevant, whereas in sadism the aim is to frighten, humiliate, and control the object, and thus the reaction of the object is crucial (Glasser, 1979). This difference is also referred to as between "self-preservative violence", where there appears to be no concern for the fate of the other, and "sadistic violence", where the victim is intended to suffer. This suffering could be seen as both exciting and as a means of communication.

Jung believed that the opposite of love was not hate, but power (Hewison, 2009), and De Masi talks of power and triumph achieved by the "total destruction" of the other, which, as it is unconscious, has to be repeated over and over again.

In my clinical experience, I have found that the triumph appears to be over the "dependency of the self" which is subjectively experienced as a state of humiliating and unbearable powerlessness. The fear is that this dependency, or "indebtedness" (to use Winnicott's term), will be inevitably exploited by the other, rather than the dependency developing into a healthy relationship of a mature, complementary, and commensurate need in the couple. Omnipotent control is then felt to be the only defence against such an other, who it is believed will otherwise inevitably abandon the subject, or cause the subject to trigger a state of total internal disintegration equivalent to the total annihilation of the self. It is the dependent self that is ultimately regarded as the cause of this constantly impending attack, and it is therefore peremptorily attacked by being treated with the utmost contempt and aggression. Inevitably, this picture is complicated by the envy which results from such a powerful projective identification on to an object, seen to be free and full of vitality.

The extent of the destruction of the other in fantasy seems to be related to problems occurring at different developmental stages, and I will argue that the resultant object relationship can be shown to reflect the level of development when the problem arose.

Couple therapists are therefore more likely to encounter this problem, especially when the "couple fit" is not so smoothly contiguous, or a difference or rift has begun to appear where previously there was agreement. In this context, I suggest the term "sexualisation" could be misleading to therapists, especially as the phenomenon can just as frequently occur in couples where there is no sex, the type of "no sex couple" described by Grier in his paper "Lively and deathly intercourse" (2009). It is important to note that "sexualisation" is used by Freud and other writers to describe an unconscious mechanism leading to excitation and not the manner of the subsequent acting out.

Clinical illustrations

In this chapter, through describing my work with two couples, I will attempt to illustrate how an unconscious sadomasochistic dynamic in the couple relationship can present in remarkably different ways, noting that the sexual element may not seem to be present in any overt form. Second, I will argue there may not always be an attempt to entirely destroy the object, but that in some cases sadism functions as a means of unconscious communication of one person's experience to their object through projective identification. Third, I have observed that what is being re-enacted through the sadomasochistic relationship is an attempt either to destroy or have total power over the dependent, vulnerable part of the self and its links to the object. The fate of the object in the real world, and therefore of the couple relationship, results from this compulsive attempt.

The two couples I refer to presented with apparently very different initial presentations. I describe their attempts to overcome what I believe at root to be somewhat similar difficulties, by using defensive strategies which overtly bear little resemblance to one another. I suggest the strategies utilised are related to the stage of development at which their extreme vulnerability and lack of containment occurred. I present a very detailed study of the work with one couple with overt sadomasochistic presentation to illustrate the development of this thought as the work progressed and will be contrasted to ongoing work with a second couple.

Both couples presented have given me permission to use the material from their therapy in this chapter, and I have taken tremendous care to disguise their identities from the external world. However, the unique and specific nature of their lives and fantasies make total anonymity impossible.

Mr and Mrs A

Mr and Mrs A came into treatment conscious of a problem in their sexual relationship which they jointly attributed to a lack of trust between them. They agreed that an interest in pornography seemed to have got out of hand, resulting in the diminution of their sexual relationship. Initially, the couple had shared in the excitement of dressing up for sex. Together they had enacted sadomasochistic fantasies, where the wife donned corsets and beat her husband with a whip. This gave them mutual satisfaction, albeit the beating was sometimes harder than requested.

There was some evidence that this behaviour had its roots in early phantasies for each which produced a convincing couple fit. Both grew up with dominant mothers. Mr A had frequently watched his sister being beaten with a riding crop by their mother, whilst he had been spared. Mrs A's mother tended to control her father, justifying this as an attempt to prevent manic swings which otherwise resulted in his hospitalisation. Both were also the favoured children in their families, and therefore attracted special attention of dubious value.

The couple regarded their mutual sexual interests as being special and different to "normal dull sex", which they associated with the parental couple. Consequently, there was no questioning authority to think about any possible transgressional element in their sexual activities.

The split in the couple collusion occurred when Mrs A became distressed upon discovering her husband watching pornography in which women were being tortured very severely. Meanwhile, there was an increase in his interest in bondage and enacting scenarios where he was either the victim of extreme pain, or playing the role of Sissy-maid (submissive male where feminisation is achieved through cross-dressing) to a female dominatrix. Mrs A also realised that the equipment and clothing were fetishistic items not merely props, and as such were more interesting to him than the person wearing them, herself.

At this point, she felt that her husband as she knew him was disappearing but also that she, as a person, was disappearing from her husband's mind. This could indicate, as De Masi suggests, the total destruction of the true "other". In the couple dynamic, I noted the attempt to convert the other to a perfect seamless fit, to destroy the otherness of the other. Mrs A wanted Mr A to be "cured", to give up the worst of this behaviour and return to the man she knew him to be, whilst Mr A wanted to convert Mrs A into someone who would understand and accept his interest as both essential to him and fundamentally harmless. At one stage, when writing up notes after a session, I inadvertently wrote the word "convertation" when I intended to say "conversation", which seemed to perfectly sum up the aim of their verbal dialogue. At this point, what had started as a collusive couple fit had become a "duet for one" whereby they seemingly had only one mind so there was no discord (Fisher, 1999), but the question was, which one? The shared fantasy was that the "other" would change to fit in with one's own need, whilst no change was required in the self.

There seemed virtually no interest in understanding the meaning of what was going on between them. My use of the word "understanding" was reduced to a function of control akin to understanding how an appliance worked in order to operate it more effectively. Indeed, there seemed to be no creative thinking, but the couple seemed to be colluding to kill off the phallic paternal function and also to attack any oedipal couple, which resembled their derided parents.

They also shared the view that the "female function" was to be totally accepting, like a mother with a new baby in a state of reverie, but this was strained to its limits as Mr A's interests became more and more extreme, and he continued to search for total acceptance whilst provoking rejection.

Unconsciously, the couple's shared fantasy seemed to involve erotising the avoidance of true intercourse, or intimacy; thence incorporating an attack on the oedipal couple which involves two different individuals, whilst simultaneously, at a developmentally much earlier level, erotising the perceived power imbalance between parent and child. Their common fantasy, that it is impossible to come together unless one person is changed to "fit in" with the other, then becomes their mutual unconscious aim (Dicks, 1967).

As the therapy progressed, Mr A's sexual acting out increased. As Mrs A refused to co-operate, Mr A needed to contact co-conspirators on the Internet with whom he would enact complex fantasies involving plentiful apparatus. His fantasies involved an intricate and ever-changing game of power, control, and domination. The sexual fantasies centred upon being in control of someone who is in control of themselves, which seemed to be a perfect description of the omnipotent phantasy of an infant in relation to its mother, but is also mirrored in the mind of the newly delivered mother who is quite shocked to discover that her life is no longer her own. More extreme complicated fantasies would involve rubber hoods and breathing tubes and ball gags that functioned to take the participants literally to the edge of life or death, an extreme re-enacting of the precarious balance between life and death of the newborn infant in the mother's hands.

All real danger was being consciously denied at this time, and the main emotional goal seemed to be achieving wholesale, unconditional acceptance. This word "acceptance" was repeated frequently during sessions and seemed to describe the type of relationship that would need to exist in Mr A's mind before he could risk moving from a paranoid-schizoid way of functioning to a more depressive way of relating, the requisite safe position from which to begin such a movement. When these fantasies took over, it was as if he disappeared into a fantasy world that resembled a dream, where there was no need for reality testing at all.

I managed to distance myself from colluding with Mrs A's omnipotent conviction that she understood entirely what this acting out was about. I asked Mr A to describe to me, in his wife's presence, the content of his enacted fantasies, and particularly the function of the equipment which he employed in his scenarios. I had previously been concerned that I might be becoming caught up in their projections, becoming in both their minds, and mine, the voyeur, viewing the pornography with him in a perverse collusion against his wife. However, I recovered my ability to be curious as I realised the images were, to me, entirely non-erotic and the equipment initially incomprehensible. Noting my countertransference lacked any erotic feeling, I became convinced that the impetus for this behaviour was not at a genital level. As Stoller says: "If the observer knew everything that had happened in the life of the person he is studying he would find these historical events represented in the details of the manifest sexual act" … he would discover "when and why the person gave up what he would most have liked erotically, to choose the alternatives that are the perversion's scenario", he added "the perversion is the scenario put into action" (Stoller, 1986, p. 425).

I found I was puzzling over a non-verbal form of communication that seemed to describe mainly sensations and primitive relationships of control, as if I were watching a dream unfold. It became obvious that Mr A was manipulating his objects and part-objects at a pre-verbal, very primitive level of development. As well as fearing my curiosity was perverse, I had also unconsciously feared that finding and using my own separate mind as an individual analyst would somehow subvert the couple perspective. This helped me understand that I was caught up in the couple dynamic where there was a huge split between extreme omnipotent certainty and the fear of knowing.

Utilising developmental theory

Mr A described searching for an extremely heightened level of sensation in some areas of his body through the technique of deadening sensation in other areas (encasing himself in rubber). He detailed the nature of the controlling relationship that he enacted, between himself and his object, in his scenarios of sadomasochism (involving "being in control of someone who was in control of oneself!"). Central to this is the extreme paradox: the person in the role of the submissive partner being tortured occupies the position of the one with the power, dictating the limits of the "game" and telling the apparently dominant actor when to stop. Put in other terms, the dependent self becomes dominant and has the power.

To my amazement, Mr A said, "it is ultimately about tenderness; the whole point is to give the submissive one a wonderful experience. It is about being very, very vulnerable." Here the dependent self is meant to be tenderly treated. (In the external world, this was a man who was overtly deeply opposed to violence.)

This extremely intricate balance of power is then enacted to its limits of tolerance. The dominant person, who is in the position of being maximally sadistic if they were to lose control, is being controlled, not from the inside but from the outside, ultimately by their wish to stay in the "game" or relationship. The ostensibly weaker/submissive partner (dependent self), paradoxically shows their strength by having the willpower to endure without flinching or collapsing under pressure, but also, according to the scenario, holds the other's precariously balanced state of mind in their own mind. This is then quite clearly an enactment of the fantasy of the vulnerability of the infant in the power of the mother. Stoller says "The masochist is never truly the victim because he never truly relinquishes control" (1986, p. 425). After these descriptions, Mrs A would say "I knew all this before", which I found hard to believe.

This couple frequently engaged at a level more related to the autistic spectrum. Tustin hypothesises that early childhood autism develops from a situation where there is an overly close relationship between the mother and child and an excluded or emotionally absent father. The mother in these cases is often depressed and the child becomes a "cork child" (McDougall, 1980, p. 420) to plug the hole in the mother's depression. The undue closeness of mother and child leads to the illusion that the child is still part of the mother's body after birth, "preventing normal attachment processes from development" (ibid.). Sudden awareness of separateness is "experienced as a death-dealing catastrophe of poignant loss" (ibid.). Autistic processes have developed as a reaction to this "unbearable elemental trauma of separateness, the deadening of responsiveness being a reaction which is specific to any kind of trauma" (Tustin, 1994, p. 2); this reminds me of Mr A's attempt to control the areas of deadening.

Tustin explains that "we all use 'sensation shapes' and 'sensation objects'. It is when they become compulsive and addictive and are used inappropriately to the exclusion of more socialised ways of dealing with sensation-driven impulses that they can be called 'autistic sensation objects'. The child's sensation has gone awry, become perverse" (Tustin ,1994, p. 8).

Chronologically, Mr A's interest evolved and accelerated from cross-dressing to the use of autistic objects following the stillbirth of the couple's only baby, leaving him with a second depressed mother, facing the final loss of her whole childbearing potential in her late forties. When this couple got together, Mr A had, I believe, been used like the "cork child" to block Mrs A's experience of the "catastrophe of poignant loss" of her previous husband, who had recently died in a road accident, a probable re-enactment of the too-sudden loss of her own mother in infancy. Tustin states that "autistic children have no fantasies and their trauma has occurred earlier ... the autism seems to provide a tough outer skin, both to protect his vulnerability and to cage his murderous violence. It is a defence against the black hole type of depression" (1994, p. 4). Interestingly, throughout the therapy, Mrs A consistently claimed she had no fantasies.

Mr A's "pornographic" interests were sensation-dominated in just this way. He liked to entirely encase his head in a rubber hood, like Bick's "second skin", that seemed to hold him together (Bick, 1968, pp. 484–486). Male chastity equipment bound and controlled his genitalia, so that nothing in terms of a response or discharge could leak out of him (no erection was possible). Here, the dependent self could not disclose its vulnerability. Gags and breathing tubes, whilst restricting his breathing, bound him against the demands of his own nature, particularly any physical manifestation of need. Sensations generated by the "other" in real human terms were rejected; kissing was "disgusting", particularly if penetration by tongues was involved; smells of the "other" were avoided at all costs. "Anything ... which is 'not me' arouses intense terror" because it reminds the infant of separation (Tustin, 1994, p. 2). Meanwhile, the sound of rustling silk was desirable and highly prized, and the sensation of silk stockings and tight Lycra were considered erotic for their own sake. "Lacking contact with people as people, such a child has little motivation to communicate in the usual way. ... all energies are concentrated on engendering a protective covering of 'me sensations' to keep the 'not me' at bay" (ibid.).

Mr and Mrs A had presented with a problem that they were deter-mined to see as a sexual problem, whereas to my mind this seemed an almost classic example of the sadomasochistic monad as described by De Masi. The object in the real world was being destroyed: Mrs A was aware that she was effectively redundant as her husband disappeared into his self-sufficient fantasy world; however, for Mr A, the excitement did not seem to emanate from the destruction of the object entirely; the internal object, or indeed part-object, had to be minutely controlled to defend against disintegration of the self. At times, Mr A had delighted in watching the torture of women on screen, mainly identifying with the tortured object playing the part of the masochist. The persecuting object was triumphed over through identification, but also the "little dependent wimp" (the dependent self) was increasingly learning to bear the torture in fantasy, so, in a perverse way, was being strength-ened, whilst the sadist who showed contempt for the dependency was identified with.

In terms of the initial couple fit, when the couple got together the needs of the "cork child" in Mr A fitted the gap for Mrs A following the loss of her previous husband, a gap that could be instantly filled. The subsequent loss of a child, however, caused Mrs A to become the depressed mother, who was no longer available and totally accepting of the needs of her dependent infant in Mr A.

Mr and Mrs H

Mr and Mrs H presented with Mrs H's addiction to alcohol, which had got totally out of control in the wake of an intensely life-endangering operation undergone by Mr H. The operation had followed twenty-five years (most of their time together) of living with a congenital, acutely life-threatening illness that had included one catastrophic near-death experience. This illness, which could be managed but not controlled, had been genetically inherited from Mr H's father, who had died suddenly when Mr H was in his early twenties. Significantly, neither the illness nor operation was mentioned until several months into the therapy.

Mrs H had a history of anorexia and bulimia dating from her early teens, during which time she had used alcohol to sustain a very high-achieving "false-self" defence (Winnicott, 1960). In the months fol-lowing her husband's operation, Mrs H's dependency on alcohol had rapidly accelerated and, to prevent its discovery, she had resorted to lies and deception.

The operation had been more traumatic for Mrs H than for her husband, who seemed to have prepared himself very thoroughly for his own quite likely death during surgery. He had a very realistic understanding of the risks involved and so had entered the operating theatre with a "what will be will be" attitude. In the lead-up to surgery, he had been entirely self-focused and largely unaware that he had ignored the potential impact on his wife and his teenage children at anything other than the practical level, for which he had provided.

The couple came into therapy when they had been living apart for nearly six months, three months of which had involved Mrs H entering a "drying out" clinic that also specialised in other addictive behaviours and eating disorders. When therapy commenced, they were considering a trial reunion and were also very concerned about the furiously angry behaviour of a teenage son. The first phase of our work together focused on the attempt to rehabilitate Mrs H into the family, whilst trying to understand the root causes of the problem. This contextual history of the operation emerged only after some months of work as the alcoholic behaviour, the acting out of the son, and Mr H's anger had been the main foci. Initially, Mrs H, who found it difficult to articulate feelings, suggested that her drinking habit was as a direct result of Mr H's inability to control and modify his angry outbursts, which reminded Mrs H of her own angry, frightening, morally controlling father and a childhood dominated by his terrifying outbursts of rage.

After about a year of once-weekly couple therapy sessions, during which Mrs H also attended regular Alcoholics Anonymous (AA) meetings and her own twice-weekly therapy, it had become difficult not to see Mrs H as the patient and Mr H as the resentful victim. Mrs H was also fairly withdrawn and unforthcoming in the sessions which led inevitably to Mr H becoming much more articulate (his only opportunity to have his psychological needs met was in the context of the couple work). He tended to dominate the sessions, complaining that Mrs H preferred the company of their son to him, leaving him feeling forgotten and neglected at home. He felt aggrieved that he had kept their home together during Mrs H's six-month absence at AA, yet now she frequently "forgot" to share significant information with him, or she would withdraw to bed or go out without explaining where she was going.

In many ways, it suited the couple to exclusively adopt the illness model with regard to alcohol abuse, as this allowed them both to become the victim; it also allowed Mr H to be the "expert" on the cure regime, in which he felt he had much professional expertise. It was very hard to establish any curiosity in the minds of the couple about any deeper meaning to the behaviour. Like with Mr and Mrs A, there seemed to be a shared omnipotent belief that they knew the underlying reason for the problem; it felt hard for me to inject curiosity into this mix.

At this point, the therapy was focused on the lack of communication and the reasons for this, and the consequential lack of intimacy and trust. Mrs H had also admitted that she wanted to have the occasional drink socially and not be controlled by the AA's total abstinence "rule". More worryingly, she had also sometimes bought and drank alcohol secretly during the day, and both these things were making Mr H feel acutely anxious, powerless, and gradually more depressed.

Each partner expressed despairing suicidal thoughts during this time, Mrs H because she identified with feeling blamed for all the problems, yet felt profoundly misunderstood, rather like Mr A, and Mr H because he felt he was made acutely anxious about his whole life situation and felt there was nothing he could now trust in Mrs H, more like Mrs A.

Mr H gradually came to recognise that he was suffering from a typical post-traumatic stress disorder, and that the years of uncertainty due to his life-threatening illness and then during Mrs H's uncontrolled drinking had been experienced by him as trauma. He was able to access his feelings of terror and hypervigilance which had been greatly increased by Mrs H's withdrawal; in the face of no meaningful communication from her, his imagination worked overtime filling the gap in information. In turn, this hypervigilance then caused him to behave in an intrusive and controlling manner that exacerbated Mrs H's withdrawal. It seemed that the powerlessness and watchfulness that had been dominant features of his own life hanging in the balance for twenty-five years had been transferred onto his anxiety about the alcoholism, and despite being highly stressed, his overt anxiety with regard to his state of health faded considerably. It was as if Mrs H was functioning as a focus for finally accessing and expressing the persecution he may have felt for years over the fear and unfairness of his illness, which he was powerless to fix.

In the sessions, as he clearly became increasingly desperate, his language towards his wife became more and more persecuting in his attempt to describe the effects his powerlessness to control her behaviour had on him; in one particular session, Mrs H seemed to be shrinking before my eyes under the onslaught of his guilt-provoking anger.

I felt utterly conflicted, realising Mr H needed to express his agony, yet I could tell that Mrs H could not bear to hear any more. I finally stopped Mr H from speaking, to ask how she was feeling, and she said "tortured". They were torturing one another in a form of totally unconscious sadistic attack, and the risk of suicide, which the psychiatric referrer had feared, was very real, both as a means of potentially punishing one another and as a means of escaping intolerable pain and uncertainty themselves. Thinking of the concept of revenge, I recognised that Mrs H, though less articulate than her husband, had been holding at bay a feeling of "torture" which was not entirely about the current situation. My countertransference took me to an association to Mr H's operation; I realised that we had in fact heard no detail about the degree to which Mrs H had suffered during this period.

Mrs H met my enquiries with a look of relief that something was finally being recognized, and I explained my thinking that she, as perceived perpetrator, had mainly suffered in silence. She then described in grotesque detail the total horror of what she had had to see and endure when visiting her half-dead husband in intensive care who may not have survived. She then looked at me and said, "Imagine what it is like when the same person dies twice". At this point, I assumed she was referring to a time when her husband had had a cardiac arrest on a walk on the cliff path, assuming that the operation then represented "the second time". This was the end of the session, and I felt we were all abandoned on the cliff edge.

The following session, however, began with another prolonged complaint about a drinking bout and another description of Mr H's feeling of unbearable anxiety, paradoxically returning to this relatively "safe ground"; it was the second session before we could take up the above reference. Then Mrs H said that the first "death" was not the cardiac arrest, as I had supposed, but an occasion in the very early stages of their courtship when Mr H had slept with an ex-girlfriend. This was a betrayal she had never forgotten and was the conscious root of her hypervigilance; her fear of annihilatory separation. As this was talked about, Mr H blushed deeply and admitted that he had known immediately that this was what was being referred to in the previous session. He reacted by defending himself, saying that in his mind the infidelity had occurred at a stage in the relationship before he was entirely committed and that he had never been unfaithful since. This reaction merely served to totally obliterate Mrs H's emotional experience in the moment. That betrayal seemed to hold and bind to it all Mrs H's experience of dependency, vulnerability, and lack of trust; it represented the "unbearable elemental trauma of separateness" (Tustin, 1994, p. 194). She could safely accuse Mr H of negligence in this, whereas the insecurity that had tortured her throughout his physical illness she would have felt too guilty about berating him for.

Meanwhile, a pattern had emerged in Mrs H's drinking episodes. Having been "dry" for over a year, and having returned to her highly responsible profession, she intermittently began to arrive home from work and give her husband a kiss, whereupon he would inevitably notice the smell of alcohol on her breath. He would ask her if she had had a drink, she would deny it, repeatedly, and after an intense interrogation would finally admit she "had had a small, quarter bottle of wine". Mr H remained doubtful that this was the extent of her drinking. (Less frequently, this would also occur on her day off, more often than not when she had seen her individual therapist.) Recognising a pattern over weeks, I began to suspect that this was linked to managing the transition between work and home, and when I suggested this she seemed startled, but agreed that this was certainly the case. Again, I noticed a relief coupled with surprise from Mrs H, as if she did not expect to be understood, only criticised.

Discussion

In working with patients with addictions, I have long been aware of the function performed by an addictive substance, particularly by alcohol, to manage transitions. In England, the rubber nipple given to a baby is called a "dummy", which accurately names the non-reality of the false nipple. In America, this is called a "soother" or "comforter" and, when overused, it frequently fails, as it offers no capacity for containment and is by definition detached from the containing function of the mother's mind. Winnicott distinguishes between "comforters", which never function fully to symbolise the mother, and "soothers", which he defines as "a sedative which always worked. ... a typical example of what I am calling a transitional object"; he also said, "most mothers allow their infants some special objects and expect them to become, as it were, addicted to such objects" (Winnicott, 1971, p. 114). However, he explains that it functions to manage the developing distinction between "me" and "not me" at a particular developmental stage; as it is within the power of the infant, it helps that infant deal with "the intermediate area between the subjective and that which is objectively perceived" (Winnicott, 1971, p. 114). The transitional object is necessary for a small child who cannot be told what is happening, at about eighteen months of age. However:

> When no understanding can be given, then when the mother is away. ... she is dead from the point of view of the child. This is what dead means ... Before the limit is reached the mother is still alive; after this limit has been overstepped she is dead. In between is a precious moment of anger, but this is quickly lost, or perhaps never experienced, always potential and carrying fear of violence.
>
> (Winnicott, 1988, p. 25)

Mrs H was terrified of that "moment of anger", as having such an explosive father, she was afraid that it would inevitably erupt into violence. Mr H had an acknowledged problem with his anger, providing a perfect couple fit. However, Mrs H was equally terrified of her own anger and instead acted out in this way, using the alcohol as "the sedative which always works" whilst also sadistically torturing her object in Mr H and simultaneously remaining "the victim" of her own alcoholic "illness" addiction.

Mrs H was attempting to manage the transitional period when she returned from work when she was trying to bring her object/mother alive again. She has a very demanding responsible job, but one she has always managed by "clothing herself" in a false self. At root, she was shy with low self-esteem, but professionally she succeeded in studying at a top institution where the motto was that "you can always tell a graduate from X, but you can't tell him anything". She admits that the combination of anorexia and alcohol helped with the construction of a false self with nearly omnipotent confidence, and it is this persona that she still robes herself in during the working day and in her social life, entering a type of bubble. In this bubble, I suspect that she has killed off her objects and her own vulnerability. On returning "home", she then faced the ambivalence of bringing her carer/mother alive again, and with it her "dependent self". Tustin describes this as living "solely in terms of outside appearances and body surfaces in order to avoid the inner unknowable darkness about which they are in despair" (Tustin, 1994, p. 276).

At the time of writing, this work is ongoing. I am currently of the opinion that there is an unconscious couple fit which fundamentally links to living on the edge of "death", both real and fantasised. At one stage in the therapy, after a public figure had died from his addiction to alcohol, Mrs H admitted she was terrified of dying herself and recognised that in many ways hers could be a similar fate. In her profession, she has to regularly deal with death, but does so in her omnipotent way, never sharing the feelings with her husband when they return from work.

I suspect that she might be concealing the full extent of her terror and that her fear of death is more like the nameless dread described by Bion caused by a catastrophic failure in containment: "If the projection is not accepted by the mother the infant feels that its feeling that it is dying is stripped of such meaning as it has. It therefore reintrojects, not a fear of dying made tolerable, but a nameless dread" (Bion, 1962, p. 308). Winnicott also describes the fear of death being the "fear of something which has already happened", like the fear of breakdown. In this context, he says, "we need to use the term 'breakdown' to describe the unthinkable state of affairs that underlies the defensive organisation" (Winnicott, 1974, p. 103) and describes it as "the original agony". "The ego organises defences against breakdown of ego organisation, and it is the ego organisation that is threatened. But the ego cannot organise against environmental failure in so far as dependence is a living fact" (ibid.).

Mr and Mrs H got together as a couple shortly after Mr H had had his terminal diagnosis, and I now think that part of the masochistic attraction from Mrs H's perspective was in living with someone who could apparently manage his own fears with regard to his omnipresent imminent mortality. I believe that this is the "living fact" of dependency and essential vulnerability which Mrs H cannot bear; the "dependent self". The experience of "original agony" is then projected onto her husband, who ironically and paradoxically then comes to have serious suicidal ideation, having spent most of his adult life trying to stay alive. It is not the real death that is feared as much as the reintrojected fear, magnified by lack of containment.

The establishment internally of a projective-identification-rejecting–object means that instead of an understanding object the infant has a wilfully misunderstanding object—with which it is identified. Further its psychic qualities are perceived by a precocious and fragile consciousness.

(Bion, 1962, p. 309)

Grier, in citing a similar clinical example, says:

It was not a case of a lack of life-instinct links. Instead something sado-masochistically perverse was attacking the life-giving links and seducing the personality with the promise of something exciting, pleasurably dangerous and destructive, both to its object and to itself. Something that might have started as a defence was beginning to develop an exciting life of its own, and was threatening to become the dominant principle of the personality.

(Grier, 2009, p. 58)

Frequently in the sessions, I felt we were re-visited by this combination of precociousness and fragility as each projects onto the other their experience of precarious, cliff-edge vulnerability and the resultant wish for sadistic revenge for their predicament. However, I think that this wish to make the other suffer seems to be a wish to communicate to the other how it really feels to be nothing but a powerless terrified puppet dangling over the cliff. Through mutual projective identification, the "dependent self" is projected, but also tortured in an enactment of identification with the omnipotent cruel parent. Mr H does not believe in any God but yet admits to having bargained with God to allow him to stay alive to have "a pint with his youngest son". At the time of referral, this son was seventeen years old. "God" is clearly the father who cannot be trusted to stay alive and protect one, but is also the best of what remains.

Conclusion

In both couples, there are emotionally disturbed mothers and weak, mentally ill, or absent fathers, and this has exacerbated the lack of containment from mother.

Mendelsohn suggests that when each member of the couple is identified with the victim, rather than one being identified with the attacker and the other with the victim, then apparently the same dynamic, that of one attacking the other, is seen. However, he suggests that in this situation the paranoid fear is in the ascendant, identifiable by a predominance of dread, and that these couples are more accurately described as paranoid-masochistic rather than sadomasochistic. He suggests that the attacks that are perpetrated are motivated predominantly by fear rather than a wish to destroy (Mendelsohn, 2014).

The work with these two couples demonstrates that beneath their very different presentations there is a common denominator of hatred towards their dependent selves. In couples where dependency is regarded by each partner with contempt, it is sadistically attacked in the other and accompanies some unconscious hope of it being tolerated and therefore understood.

References

Bick, E. (1968). The experience of the skin in early object relationships. *International Journal of Psycho-Analysis, 49*: 484–486.

Bion, W. R. (1962a). The psycho-analytic study of thinking. *International Journal of Psycho-Analysis, 43*: 306–310.

Bion, W. R. (1962b). *Learning from Experience.* London: Karnac.

Britton, R. (1998). Before and after the depressive position. In: *Belief and Imagination* (pp. 69–106). London: Routledge, New Library of Psychoanalysis.

De Masi, F. (2003). *The Sado-Masochistic Perversion: The Entity and the Theories.* Trans. P. Slotkin. London: Karnac.

Dicks, H. (1967). *Marital Tensions.* London: Maresfield.

Fisher, J. V. (1999). Duet for one? Two people or a couple. In: *The Uninvited Guest: Emerging from Narcissism towards Marriage* (pp. 78–104). London: Karnac.

Freud, S. (1920g). *Beyond the Pleasure Principle. S. E., 18:* 3–64. London: Hogarth.

Freud, S. (1924c). The economic problem of masochism. *S. E., 19*: 157–170. London: Hogarth.

Glasser, M. (1979). Some aspects of the role of aggression in the perversions. In: I. Rosen (Ed.), *Sexual Deviation* (pp. 278–306). Oxford: Oxford University Press.

Grier, F. (2009). Lively and deathly intercourse. In: *Sex, Attachment and Couple Psychotherapy* (pp. 44–61). London: Karnac.

Hewison, D. (2009). Power vs love in sadomasochistic couple relations. In: *Sex, Attachment and Couple Psychotherapy* (pp. 165–185). London: Karnac.

Joseph, B. (1971). A clinical contribution to the analysis of a perversion. *International Journal of Psycho-Analysis, 52*: 441–449.

Laplanche, J., & Pontalis J.-B. (1985). *The Language of Psycho-Analysis*. London: Hogarth.

McDougall, J. (1980). A child is being eaten II: the abysmal mother and the cork child—a clinical illustration. *Contemporary Psychoanalysis, 16*: 417–459.

Mendelsohn, F. (2014). Revisiting the sadomasochistic marriage: the paranoid masochistic relationship. *Psycho-Analytic Review, 101*: 647–673.

Parens, H. (1997). The unique pathenotricity of sexual abuse. *Psychoanalytic Enquiry, 17*: 250–266.

Perelberg, R. J. (1999). The interplay between identifications and identity in the analysis of a violent young man. *International Journal of Psycho-Analysis, 80*: 31–45.

Stoller, R. J. (1974). Hostility and mystery in perversion. *International Journal of Psycho-Analysis, 55*: 425–433.

Stoller, R. J. (1986). *Perversion: The Erotic Form of Hatred*. London: Karnac Classics.

Tustin, F. (1994). *Autistic Barriers in Neurotic Patients*. London: Karnac.

Winnicott, D. W. (1960). Ego distortions in terms of the true and false self. In: *The Maturational Process and the Facilitating Environment*. London: International University Press.

Winnicott D. W. (1969). Transitional objects and transitional phenomena. In: *Playing and Reality*. London: Pelican Books.

Winnicott, D. W. (1971). The location of cultural experience. In: *Playing and Reality*. London: Pelican Books.

Winnicott, D. W. (1974). Fear of breakdown. *International Review of Psycho-Analysis, 21*: 103–107.

CHAPTER EIGHT

Sadomasochism in the context of family relationships

John Miller

Introduction

At one stage in my life, I did a lot of work as a psychological consultant to various private organisations that catered for children with learning and behaviour problems. These organisations seemed driven by the financial possibilities of catering for children whom nobody wanted, and were staffed with people seemingly motivated by unresolved personal issues which I imagined might have hampered their ability to sustain a job in mainstream education. I was therefore pleasantly surprised when a group of schools to which I was consultant appointed a new head of care who struck me as being educated, intelligent, and psychologically stable. We immediately hit it off, and I looked forward to an enjoyable working partnership. After a while, he expressed his wish to have an analysis with me. However, after explaining the boundary conflicts, I referred him on to trusted colleagues; I later learned he had not pursued this matter further.

As our working partnership flourished, and our personal fondness for each other grew, I invited him and his partner for lunch with my wife and I at our home one weekend. The four of us got along very well and we enjoyed their visit very much.

A couple of weeks later, when term was due to start, I contacted the head office wanting to leave a message for this man. "Haven't you heard?", the secretary exclaimed in dismay, "he's dead!" It appeared that my colleague and new-found friend had been stabbed to death by his partner, apparently in self-defence.

I do not know what actually happened, and I was unable to follow the court case that took place some distance from where I lived. However, I have since come to the conclusion that an extreme degree of splitting or dissociation must have been operating within this couple for them to be able to give such a convincing impression of rational, adult functioning and emotional warmth, and yet be so incapable of managing their aggression that they lapsed into such primitive behaviour. I have since come to understand this as an extreme example of sadomasochism.

Theoretical background

Freud originally thought of masochism as aggression turned in on itself (1915). By 1919 Freud observed that patients reported fantasies, when being beaten as a child, that there was another child, somewhere, being beaten. This other child was phantasied to be a hated, rival sibling being beaten (to death). Through the unconscious delusion that they were this other child, they were able to take pleasure in the actual beating they were receiving.

This was the beginning of understanding projective identification, a term later formulated by Melanie Klein in her paper entitled "Notes on some schizoid mechanisms" (1946). Klein described how the baby, in its primitive mental functioning, artificially splits experiences with the mother into all-good and all-bad categories. The all-bad experiences are disowned or evacuated by unconsciously projecting these into mother. This artificial splitting is the schizoid element, and the attributing of anything bad or unpleasant to someone outside oneself (the mother) constitutes the paranoid element—hence the term "paranoid-schizoid position" (Klein, 1946). Through this mechanism, the baby creates the illusion that a major part of its experience belongs to the mother. In doing so, the baby can harbour the delusional fantasy of having taken control of—or even of becoming—mother.

Klein originally conceived of projective identification as being purely pathological. She said, "Much of the hatred against parts of the self is now directed towards the mother. This leads to a particular form of identification which establishes the prototype of an aggressive object relation. I suggest that these processes are described by the term 'projective identification'" (Klein 1946, pp. 99–110). Bion realised that, universal though these pathological mechanisms might be, they actually involved the misuse or distortion of the healthy and necessary process through which all emotional development has to take place at the start of life. The baby being, as the British poet Lord Tennyson put it, "with no language but a cry" (Tennyson, 1849, stanza 54), can only relate to its mother by somehow putting its discomfort and distress into her non-verbally. It is when things go seriously wrong with this exchange that pathological projective identification is set up (Bion, 1962).

In adult life, projective identification can involve the delusional fantasy of having become somebody else. This can take the form of imagining oneself to be an actual person, a common example being the way in which people in the early stages of analysis will often tend to unconsciously impersonate the analyst in the relationships in the outside world. More commonly, perhaps, it takes the form of living the delusion of being some kind of figure—everybody's Mother, the Hero, or the Saviour being typical examples. The crucial issue about these states of mind in which the person unconsciously projects massively, for example in disowning knowing about their own needs and unconsciously locating their own needy self in another, is that they can become overly responsive to the other's needs, or relate to an imagined (not real) other.

Sadomasochism

I believe sadomasochism can flourish in circumstances where there is an emotional vacuum created by the absence of parental containment and warm interest. This creates fertile ground for muddled early infantile ideas of possessiveness, control, and gratification. This template, based on a mother–baby dynamic as seen from an infant's perspective, can provide a pattern for subsequent partnerships in adulthood.

For instance, the average four-year-old's idea of "being Mummy" is either kissing and feeding the baby or telling it off. Four-year-olds left to keep an eye on an actual baby will sometimes do something to make the baby cry so that they can then comfort it with a kiss. Here, a primitive notion of relationships based on observation appears uninformed by emotional experience. It is also easy to imagine how an adult who has developed no further emotionally than this stage can form the idea that intimate relationships are based on a sadomasochistic dynamic where the other is someone who is yours to command and control, or vice versa.

Thus, it is conceivable that in the artificial splitting of a person into either being a sadist or a masochist, we can see that when someone behaves masochistically or sadistically, they are showing one side of the coin. At any moment, however, and without warning, the coin can flip and the masochist can become the sadist.

Aetiology

I have come to the conclusion that it is quite useful to think of sado-masochism and perversion as operating along a spectrum. Although I have never seen any reference to this elsewhere, my clinical impressions lead me to believe the perverse part of the personality can often become activated accidentally. A rather quiet, introverted parent has a child with a particularly feisty or reactive temperament. One day, the toddler is being unusually uncooperative about going to bed and protests by throwing himself about in a tantrum. In the process, he bangs his head on the door-frame, causing a small cut. Suddenly, the exasperated parent is full of concern. For a moment, the toddler is bewildered. Why has Mummy suddenly become so nice when she was being so cross just before? Aha! It is because I hurt myself! At that moment, a thought might form in the child's mind along the lines: *All I have to do in order to get away with things is to engineer a situation where I am injured and all is forgiven!* This is the child who may then go on to prefer to be shouted at or hit by adults rather than be ignored.

Julia

Many masochists have grown up in a family culture of masochism. For example, a patient of mine, Julia (not her real name) came for analysis because she was exhausted by the way her life was in chaos and seemed to lurch from one crisis to the next. She was a talented writer who had married a film producer of her father's age. At the time she presented for analysis, Julia had somehow managed to overcome her masochism sufficiently to escape from her possessive and irrational husband, with whom she had been marooned abroad, and come to Britain to start life as a single parent with the couple's seven-year-old daughter. Julia's own parents had a deeply sadomasochistic partnership, her mother being endlessly loyal to a man who sounded by turns psychotic and autistic; mother was also described as apparently in thrall to her own ninety-year-old mother. Ten years into the analysis, Julia could still not bring herself to get a divorce despite knowing it was the only thing that would shatter her husband's delusional belief that she still belonged to him. Meanwhile, their daughter went on being masochistically exposed to her totally self-obsessed father.

Basil

Basil, another patient, also came from a seemingly sadomasochistic family background. His father, a, fundamentalist pastor in the Bible Belt of America, had a long history of bipolar disorder. Basil described his father plunging into suicidal depression when he believed he had not saved enough souls; once, when Basil was naughty (at the age of about six) his father had threatened him with a loaded revolver. Basil described his mother as slavishly bound to her husband's commands. She sadistically disciplined Basil using (perhaps with unconscious symbolic irony) a metal fly swat. Basil's own marriage took the form of doing a deal with a woman who provided a house in return for financial security and the possibility of children. Being unable to see much beyond the goods and services aspect of life, he failed to register how emotionally disturbed she was. One morning, at a point when the marriage had reached a critical point of collapse, Basil came to a session looking more than usually haggard and reported that his wife had threatened to cut his throat when he was asleep. He had called the police, who had evidently taken the situation very seriously. It was perhaps a combination of the effects of the analysis and the awakening of loving instincts in him by the birth of his sons that mobilised him to get custody of them after the divorce.

Other issues of pathology

At the more perverse end of the spectrum are those who have given up on relationships. They tend cynically to ridicule love and emotion, destroying it where it seems to be flourishing. The core of it seems to involve the surrender to, and even glorification of, power and control at the cost of attacking or destroying what is good and true. This is Milton's Satan who would "Rather rule in Hell then serve in Heaven" (Milton, I, lines 262–263).

I once saw a teenage offender who was due to appear in court. In view of his delinquent history, it seemed very likely that he would be sent to a detention centre. This was a prospect that even the most hardened delinquents viewed with apprehension, but not him. "To be honest with you", he said to me, stretching his legs with a nonchalant yawn, "I prefer it. The alternative would be a fine and the detention centre will save me the money!" Here we have the heart of the matter: no one could discipline or punish him, because whatever they did, he liked it. He viewed himself as being above the law.

Once it is understood how the fate of the child (whether internal or external) is the key issue in sadomasochism, it becomes apparent that we are addressing not just emotional development but the fundamentals of morality and ethics. The child is the future. The child personifies life, creativity, spontaneity, goodness, and innocence. Producing children (whether of flesh and blood or conceptual) and protecting and caring for them is in the service of the life force and what is good. Neglecting, beating, and murdering children (fleshly or otherwise) is attacking goodness and life itself. In traditional fairy tales, those invaluable hand-books to psychological development, the witch in "Hansel and Gretel", a story written by the Grimm brothers Jakob and Wilhelm in 1812, does not kill children, she eats them (*Grimm's Fairy Tales*, 1975). Symbolically, the difference is crucial. In fairy tales and dreams, what has died or been cut off can grow or come to life again. Eating or devouring children means obstructing or aborting growth and development. Thus, when Hansel and Gretel manage to push the witch into her own oven, this is no sadistic act of revenge. The children she has previously caught and who have been turned into gingerbread are restored to life, since cooking is a process of transformation and the child victims who were previously gingerbread—something that could be "naughty-but-nice", akin to an empty indulgence—regain their potential for life and growth. Humperdinck's operatic treatment of the story (1893) vividly conveys the witch as the sadistic aspect of the masochistic mother who has aban-doned her babies to their fate in the outside world of the forest.

The killing of the child and the aborting of potential growth is the satanic heart of sadomasochism. We are increasingly aware, nowadays, of how many actual children are abused, tortured, and even murdered, but it is important to start with the awareness of how in sadomasochism the inner child—the healthy part of the personality that can grow and develop—is *always* to some extent sacrificed. This is why any psychotherapy that does not address the destructive part of the personality is bound to end up colluding with it.

At the heart of it all is the elephant in the room: sexuality. It can be unwanted, too costly to maintain, and almost impossible to get rid of. It is symptomatic of the growing problem of concreteness and lack of symbolic thinking that sexuality has come to be equated with behaviour or activity. In fact, of course, sexuality is a core aspect of human experience from babyhood to old age. We may think of a spectrum between the baby sexuality of warmth and skin contact to the spiritual sexuality of old age—perhaps exemplified by the love of Eloise and Abelard, two lovers who lived in Paris in the twelfth century (Abelard, 2004). In the middle of the spectrum lie all the experiences of passionate attachment, longing and belonging, generosity and possessiveness which preoccupy us throughout life under the heading of Love. Sexuality is, if anything, a language and, like words, it can be used to connect and relate, or to dominate and attack. It is all a question of how far a person's sexuality has evolved an adult capacity or remained infantile and narcissistic.

Adult sexuality involves *making* love: making it available, each to the other. It is a mutual act of giving. Infantile sexuality is *having* sex: of gratification, akin to eating ice cream perhaps. When two people are incapable of emotional closeness, being together becomes boring, even claustrophobic, and the obvious solution is excitement. This automatically opens the door to perversion, and as with any addiction, stronger and stronger doses are needed to fill the emotional vacuum. One of the most striking experiences of the reality of the maternal transference I have witnessed in recent years is the way in which male patients who are obsessed with the sadomasochism of pornography can find its grip on them loosen once they genuinely start to feel a real emotional connection with their analyst.

Clinical illustrations

One of the biggest issues in every analysis is how far the patient (like the child with its parent) cooperates with the process, or how far they resist or even try to sabotage it. Sadomasochism and perversion manifests itself most clearly in the dedicated stance of resistance or attempts to attack the analysis and the analytical parents. While psychological problems are undoubtedly often caused by neglect and abuse, they are just as much the product of inherently perverse attitudes in the child that consistently rubbishes the parents so that they are perceived as bad, as well as provoking them into actual negativity.

Tom

I would like to illustrate this with some material of a man in his early sixties—I will call him Tom—who came for analysis because of severe bouts of panic and anxiety. In the initial consultation, I suggested, as I almost routinely do with new patients, that he should try and hold on to the idea that everything I said was intended for his good, even if it seemed at the time to be hostile or incomprehensible. Immediately, Tom became angry and frightened. It made him deeply suspicious and fearful, he said, that I seemed to be telling him he *must* believe I was good. He felt this was sanctimonious and self-righteous. Almost immediately, a sadomasochistic dynamic started to develop where he was by turns suspicious and contemptuous of my motives while I felt increasingly abused and attacked. This was how Tom's contrariness and perverse attempt to twist everything became apparent from the very beginning. The first couple of years of the analysis felt like a kind of civil war where I, as the analytical parent, was being endlessly attacked, and meanwhile *he* felt anxious and persecuted—mainly, I think, because of the fear of the punishment or reprisals he may unconsciously have expected his attacks invited.

The first theme, which began to emerge in his dreams, was of babies and small children whom he had to rescue heroically from dangerous or unreliable mothers. After a long while, these began to be interspersed with more shocking images of children who had been injured or abused, where no mother was in the picture. Gradually, I was able to get Tom to contemplate reluctantly the possibility that these dreams said something about the way *he* abused the child part of *himself*. Some two and a half years into the analysis, he had the following dream:

> He was in a war situation crawling along a muddy trench with other soldiers in battle-dress and armed, in what seemed to be a front-line position. They were concealed from the enemy by the smoke of battle. Suddenly, all the smoke cleared, leaving him and his fellow combatants exposed to view and he was terrified that they would be immediately attacked and annihilated.

As I understood the dream, it seemed to me that the enemy was the authorities or the parents—in other words, in transference to me, the analyst. The dreamer, Tom, was the infant Tom in company with the other infant parts of himself which was busy in its resistance movement against the parents. The smokescreen that had previously been keeping this hidden corresponded to the smoke of battle which Tom repeatedly stirred up by provoking quarrels and arguments in his sessions (for which he generally tended to hold me responsible). The smokescreen cover had suddenly disappeared because I had recently been pointing out to him the way in which he was always trying to get into a fight with me in order not to have to confront anything painful or uncomfortable about himself.

A later dream provides detailed material about his pseudo-maturity and attacks on the parental couple:

> His spectacles were broken: one lens was shattered in a jagged pattern and part of the frame was missing so that it did not hold the other lens. He set off to go to the optician, but then instead seemed to be upstairs in a bus where the spectacles had broken and he thought he saw a couple who had picked up the bits he needed.

His main association to the dream was that the jagged way in which the lens had broken reminded him of a scene from the film *Vanishing Point* (1971) in which there is the shot of a jagged mountain peak being reflected in the dark glasses of a policeman. It further reminded him of an episode of an adult animated sitcom television series where a joke was made quoting this film image.

Here, it seemed to me, we had all the elements laid bare of the perverse attacks on the parental couple. His broken spectacles indicated his flawed view of the world and lack of insight. Their getting broken on the top floor of a bus seemed to be a reference to how much he tended to rely intellectually (the top floor) on collective beliefs and attitudes (the word "bus" being short for "omnibus", meaning "for everybody") and the couple who picked up the missing bits he needed were presumably a glimpse of the parents who had got hold of what he seemed to be missing. The image of the policeman with the mountain peaks reflected in his mirror glasses sounded to me like a slightly sinister or derogated view of the parents' relationship: the enigmatic, authoritarian Daddy-policeman who had an eye for Mummy's twin peaks despite their being jagged, that is, inhospitable, possibly indicating a fantasy of some kind of kinky parental sexual intercourse. It also suggested the authoritarian policeman analyst who mirrored him but would not reveal what he (the analyst) was thinking. All of this itself became the object of a mocking reference from the manic, black humour of the televised adult animated cartoon series. The optician to whom he obviously should have gone straight away to get his glasses mended seemed, in transference, to be the analyst, but he quickly abandoned this in favour of chasing after the couple to recover the missing bits. There is quite a lot packed into this little detail too. He was not turning to the couple (the parents) to repair his spectacles any more than he was going to the optician. The implication seemed to be that he could see perfectly well before, but some accident had just temporarily interrupted this, and he can sort it out himself if only he can find the missing bits.

The details of the damage to his spectacles were very informative. One lens (I think it was the lens corresponding to the left eye, which would suggest connections with the feminine, relating, and the unconscious) was shattered in a jagged pattern which in his mind was associated with the mountain peak reflected in the policeman's mirror shades. The fact of its being shattered suggested irreparable damage: it was quite unusable and would have to be replaced. I interpreted this to be symbolic of an entrenched, perverse viewpoint that had to be completely given up if he were to be able to start seeing what relationships were really about. The other lens was intact and usable, but he could not use it until the frame that held it in was repaired or replaced. If this is the right-hand side, it implies his capacity for conscious thinking, decision-making, logos, which was, indeed, intact—his successful career in industry was evidence of the fact—but in the way he thought about life, and particularly personal relationships, he couldn't frame these properly. He couldn't see things in context.

Over time, through patiently identifying, demonstrating, and challenging his perverse attacks on the parental couple, we began to notice a real softening in his personality. My blood pressure remained normal throughout most sessions, and Tom's disappointment at what an appalling analyst I had been at the beginning was replaced with admiration for how much I had improved in only a few years! He began to be able to receive my comments and interpretations, although his most fulsome response continued to be "I am sure there is a lot of truth in that!"

The capacity for intimate relationships cannot develop without first experiencing the child's relationship of good dependency. Similarly, the

capacity to learn cannot develop without the understanding and acceptance of the fact that knowledge can only be acquired from someone
else who is already knowledgeable, through a learning relationship
with them. It follows that covert derogation of the parental function
can be expected to be found underlying most relationship and learning
problems.

Lucia

Another vivid example of this was provided by a much more coopera-
tive, and less perverse, woman patient. Lucia was a twenty-six-year-old
high-flying executive in the commercial world who had great difficulty
finding and sustaining intimate relationships. One day, in a session, she
burst out with a nervous laugh, "I have this terribly embarrassing fantasy that I suppose I must tell you!" The fantasy was that she would
come to an analytical session, take off all her clothes, and masturbate
in front of me. What struck me as the most significant thing about this
fantasy was that it was all about excluding me. What she fantasised
was giving herself the experience of somehow *being* the parents having
intercourse with each other and making me the voyeur, thus revers-
ing her experience of being the child excluded from the parents' intimacy. (Significantly, she was an only child.) This brave revelation and
the detailed exploration of the infantile fantasies involved seemed to
bring about a significant change in Lucia's analysis. The delicious party
girl, preoccupied endlessly with being the object of attention, began to
be replaced by a more thoughtful and sincere young woman who was
becoming deeply attached to her analytical parents and even found a
new appreciation for her actual, well-intentioned but emotionally challenged parents back home.

Discussion

During the long years of Tom, Julia, and Basil's analyses, I found myself
constantly battling in my countertransference with the hopeless feeling
that I was masochistically banging my head against a brick wall. I had
to struggle to hold a balance between the urge to sadistically abort the
analysis, on the one hand, and masochistically to allow the material to
wash over me without attempting to come to grips with it. Like every
patient in analysis, to some extent, the sadomasochist is torn between

the healthy desire to be rescued from their perverse states and the perverse desire to drag the analyst down with them. Perhaps the most common challenge (which is for the hallmark of sadomasochism) is the way
the patient is always trying to set up an endless game of the sort that
Eric Berne (1964) called "Why don't you. ... Yes but". The patient presents the analyst with endless insoluble problems or hopeless situations
in their life with the intention, not of getting some help or understanding, but of making the analyst feel as hopeless and helpless as they do.
Coupled with this may be apparent confessions of passivity, stupidity,
or cowardice involving a tacit invitation to the analyst to beat them by
giving them an exciting "tongue-lashing".

When it comes to the question of transference, since projective identification is the very essence of sadomasochism, such patients tend to
be chronically in projective identification. Consequently, there is no real
transference in the sense of any emotional attachment to the analyst.
There is communication, but this does not take the form of a sharing of
personal experience but a violent projecting of disowned and undigested
emotional experience into the analyst. In this sense, almost everything
occurs through the countertransference in the same way that the baby
makes the mother feel the distress for which it has no words.

With such patients, there is a particularly high risk of acting in the
countertransference.

Conclusion

Sadomasochism is by its very nature two-faced and trades on deceit.
Consequently, it is most often in dreams that the deviousness of the
sadomasochistic mission to subvert good authority becomes most
apparent.

The state of the inner world is what governs each person's relationships, values, and attitudes to life. The way the patient in analysis
spontaneously responds to and experiences the analyst, and the picture
reflected in his or her dreams, are the main revelations of the state of
his or her inner world. The heart of the inner world is the relationship
between the parents, and between the parents and the child part of the
personality. Most emotional and psychological problems have their
origin in unresolved problems in the family life of the inner world, so
that analysis can be thought of as a kind of family therapy of the inner
family. This comes about through a real emotional experience of good

parenting in the analytical relationship. The more the patient has a real, living sense of good parents who have a loving and creative relationship and of being happily dependent on that experience, the more he or she will be capable of love, generosity, and intimate relationships. As it has been said, "It is never too late to have a happy childhood".

Much of the work of analysis involves a re-parenting project whereby deficiencies and confusions in early life are remedied and healed through the analytical experience. This was summed up by Freud who, in a letter to Jung, defined psychoanalysis as "in essence a cure through love" (Bettelheim, 1984).

Summary

Everyone has a perverse part of their personality that tries to attack development and relationships in the interests of self-glorification and power. Whenever someone has difficulties with intimate relationships, there is a danger that this perverse part becomes harnessed to self-justification and indulging in problems rather than trying to solve them. Sadomasochism involves states of identity confusion that particularly centre around seeing and presenting oneself as innocent victim in order to be secretly in charge and, if necessary, the justified persecutor. Many of the most common psychological problems: anxiety states, panics, and particularly relationship difficulties, originate in sadomasochistic and perverse dynamics which will only thrive if they are swept under the carpet with the aid of medication or a sympathetic chat.

It is difficult to see how the growing tide of child abuse and domestic violence can be stemmed, or indeed the exponential increase in everyday psychological problems, without a much greater attempt to understand the meaning of emotional experience with the depth of insight that psychoanalysis makes possible. The increasing trend to see everything as a question of management results merely in masochistic sticking-plasters that evade the question of adult responsibility.

References

Abelard, P. (2012). *The Letters of Abelard and Eloise*. London: Penguin.
Berne, E. (1964). *Games People Play: The Psychology of Human Relations*. New York: Grove.
Bettelheim, B. (1984). *Freud and Man's Soul*. New York: Vintage.

Bion, W. R. (1962). *Learning from Experience*. London: Heinemann.

Briggs, S. (2014). Jury convict 19-year-old man of murdering toddler Amina Agboola. *Peterborough Telegraph*, 9 September.

Freud, S. (1905d). *Three Essays on the Theory of Sexuality. S. E., 7*. London: Hogarth.

Freud, S. (1915c). Instincts and their vicissitudes. *S. E., 14*. London. Hogarth.

Freud, S. (1919e). A child is being beaten. *S. E., 10*. London: Hogarth.

Hoeller, S. A. (2012). *The Gnostic Jung and the Seven Sermons to the Dead*. Wheaton, IL: Quest Books.

Jung, C. G. (1916). *Collected Papers on Analytical Psychology*. Ed. C. E. Long. London: Bailliere, Tindal and Cox.

Klein, M. (1946). Notes on some schizoid mechanisms. *International Journal of Psycho-Analysis, 27*: 99–110.

Meltzer, D. (1992). *The Claustrum*. Strathtay, Perthshire: Clunie.

CHAPTER NINE

Sadism in later life: an unexpected dynamic?

Sandra Evans

Introduction

Sadism is not a word that sits easily with traditional images of ageing. This fact is likely to be more an effect of the sanitised and objectifying images of older people in society than any reality of the older man or woman on the street. The range of human encounters amongst the elderly are as numerous and varied as those amongst younger people, and can be occasionally tinged with negativity and the darker side of the human psyche. This chapter sets out to explore a range of interactions that involve some element of sadism and that risk going unnoticed because the sadism may be unsuspected or unseen. The risk is that if sadism is unrecognised or unacknowledged, it may go unchallenged, and consequently the potential for harm will be greater.

In this chapter, I draw upon my clinical experience of working as a consultant psychiatrist and psychotherapist/group analyst in various clinical settings within London and the South East. The clinical vignettes I present do not refer to any one person or situation but are an amalgamation of facts I have collated through my encounters between patients and their families, patients and their carers, and patients and their clinicians. Presenting clinical material in this way protects the identities of people involved whilst remaining faithful to the constellation of factors that illustrate the thrust of what I wish to convey.

Sadism, aggression, and the death drive

Sadism is the wilful hurting or humiliation of others while drawing pleasure from the knowledge and experience of their suffering. Sadism is often linked to sexual pleasure (Krafft-Ebing, 1886), and there is no reason to dismiss an erotic element to sadistic expression in older people just because they are older. The erotic may be less obvious, but in my clinical experience it is still there. Freud (1905d) described sadistic behaviour generally as an aspect of male aggression, and in part as the humiliation and maltreatment of the object. Masochism, the contrasting desire, is linked to shame and disgust in opposition to the libido (Freud, 1905d, pp. 158–159).

Later on, Freud hinted at the existence of a death drive, which perhaps is more relevant to the subject of ageing (Freud, 1920g). The notion of a death instinct was in opposition to the life instinct, and Freud described its goal as balancing the erotic, libidinal drive by bringing the organism back to the inorganic. In this, he seemed to be suggesting that the death drive is linked to destructiveness and to begin with may be depressive and directed towards the self. However, it is suggested (Laplanche & Pontalis, 1973) that this was not yet primary masochism. The death drive is subsequently in part turned outwards towards the world in the form of libidinal aggressive or destructive instincts, and this situation was equated by Freud with primary masochism, whilst perhaps acknowledging that a considerable sadistic attitude remains in play and may not subsequently be turned on the self in a secondary masochistic attack (Laplanche & Pontalis, 1973, p. 403).

Sadism, however, is not the same as aggression. Aggression can be a life instinct understood to be linked with the drive for survival. Non-human animals are aggressive and destructive when hunting for food or protecting their young. Sadism, by contrast, involves an identification with the prey and requires some intimacy to be present between the two in order for the self to appreciate the disturbance caused in the other. The difference between aggression and sadism might be illustrated by the contrast between stabbing someone in the back versus stabbing them in the gut while holding eye contact and twisting the knife. The perpetrator appears to want something from the victim, even if it is just the acknowledgement of their existence and power.

The sadistic attitude

In psychoanalytic thought, this kind of sadistic attitude is thought to have been spawned in early childhood during a disturbance within the relationship with the primary caregiver, usually the mother. Klein (1946) described how early infantile, part-object relating is filled with aggression rooted in defensiveness and rage. In illustrating the paranoid-schizoid position, she described how the absence of mother's breast is experienced by the infant as an attack on its very existence; in response, the infant might counter this felt attack by biting, for instance. Here, the infant almost literally bites the hand/breast/part-object that feeds it. Development of a mature state of mind comes with the realisation that the attacked breast is also part of the loved and desired mother. This realisation is accompanied by regret and guilt—the so-called depressive position (Klein, 1946).

Sadism exists within the context of a relationship

I have often wondered how sadism might differ from ordinary cruelty. The literature suggests that the difference is concerned with intimacy (Ruczyczynski, 2007). Somehow the need to relate to the object is thwarted or perverted and intimacy becomes tainted with the need to control the object through inflicting pain or suffering. As I understand it, ordinary cruelty can be exercised at a distance and can be a careless act; in that the perpetrator of cruelty does not appear to have a need to see or care what happens to the victim, such as the plight of civilian refugees during a war. By contrast, the sadist cares deeply. Sadism appears to be a strange kind of love, one that is still demanding of reciprocity, albeit a controlled and complicated reciprocity.

Ambivalence is a normal human experience. It is an oscillation between love and hate and is a delicate balance within most long-term relationships. Ambivalence is tempered in adults by a sense of responsibility and mutuality in interpersonal relationships. Enduring relationships are those in which partners can negotiate and survive ambivalence, difference, and conflicting needs. Individuals who, for whatever reason, have experienced profound disruption in that first dyadic relationship with mother may find difficulties with future relating when they wish to get close and yet struggle to get their needs met.

This chapter focuses on sadism within relationships for older people in three contexts. I will describe people who have long had a sadistic attitude within their relationships and who have simply grown older; people who have become sadistic or more sadistic as they deal with the vicissitudes of later life and illness; and those situations when patients or vulnerable older people are dealt with sadistically in a clinical/care setting. I hope that shedding some light on these different types of situations will enhance our understanding of sadism in later life, thus leading to a reduction in harm in this population.

Jake

Jake, a man in his late sixties, sought therapy because he was troubled by his difficulty in sustaining relationships throughout his life. He was without many friends and finally had admitted to himself that he was lonely. During encounters with people at work and also whilst trying to befriend people on online dating websites, he found himself filled with rage in response to experiencing injustice. Women came in for more criticism than men, although his object choice was men.

During therapy, it emerged that when Jake was four months old, his mother had abandoned him to the care of her in-laws. He himself was unaware of much in terms of early memories, but his father's family had filled in various details for him.

Jake's therapist happened to be a slightly overweight woman who was older than him. Following a break in therapy, Jake would make overtly disparaging remarks about old people who were fat and lazy. His therapist contextualised Jake's use of language as an expression of his aggression, in response to the break, where it seemed as if he had experienced the break as a sadistic attack by the therapist on him and his vulnerable loneliness.

Discussion

Jake was a lonely man who had desperately longed for a satisfying relationship with another person. However, he also appeared hugely ambivalent about this and seemed to eschew relating with another. So when he was offered the chance of closeness, for instance upon resuming therapy after a break, he responded with rage.

The above example illustrates how Jake behaved in a sadistic, attacking way towards his therapist in response to his perception that when she went on her breaks, she had abandoned him deliberately, despite knowing he was lonely. At such times, he experienced her departure as a sadistic attack by her on his vulnerabilities. It is worth mentioning here that he did not present as having a persistently sadistic attitude towards the therapist during the course of the therapy; a sadistic attitude seemed to surface at points when he had to manage overwhelming feelings that got stirred up internally in response to being separated from the object he depended upon.

Miriam

Miriam, a woman in her mid-seventies, suffered from long-standing difficulties with interpersonal relating. She had always struggled with relationships and had not achieved intimacy with a partner of either gender for many years. She suffered from many physical health problems, including a severely bronchitic chest that rendered her breathless and wheezy a lot of the time. She was ill with chest infections several times a year and used many inhaled medications that caused palpitations, thus adding to her feelings of anxiety. (A tachycardia and shortness of breath can induce feelings of intense anxiety in patients, so that much so that co-morbidity occurs with diseases of the airways.) Miriam called upon her general practitioner (GP) more than most patients, and often her GP felt that his consultations with Miriam were hard to end. She did not seem to pick up on normal cues suggesting the end of the consultation, and often would remove not just her coat but also her cardigan just as he would be about to wrap up the appointment. This doctor was aware that Miriam's dragging out of her appointment time was eating into the time allotted for the next patient. Yet his efforts to be fair and justifiably end Miriam's consultations after he had attended to her were met by Miriam's complaints that he was depriving her of life itself.

The GP was aware that Miriam had formed a strong attachment to him and that she disliked seeing any of the other doctors in the practice: she had informed him about each of these other doctors' failings. For their part, the other doctors had expressed relief that he, and not they, was seeing Miriam regularly, as she could be quite implacably demanding of them during consultations. This made the GP feel unsupported and cornered.

Miriam was highly complimentary about her GP and, although she was more than thirty years his senior, she behaved in a somewhat flirtatious manner towards him. The GP's visible discomfort at these moments seemed to encourage Miriam further, and she would go on to make personal comments about his physique. Appropriately, the GP began to invite the practice nurse as chaperone during Miriam's appointments. He also began to notice he was starting to anticipate Miriam's appointments with anxiety. So much so that one night he awoke with a disturbing dream in which he dreamt he was being seduced by Miriam, all the while feeling helpless.

As part of his continuing professional development, this GP attended a Balint group with peers who were not his surgery colleagues. Balint groups are named after the psychoanalyst Michael Balint (1896–1970) who, in the late 1950s, along with his wife Enid, began holding psychological training seminars for GPs in London. There were no lectures and the doctors' education was based on case presentation and small group discussions led by a psychoanalytic psychotherapist.

During the Balint group discussions, Miriam's GP described feeling that he was treading on eggshells when dealing with her, most particularly whenever there was a lack of physical symptoms suggestive of illness commensurate with her complaints of being unwell. Instead of feeling reassured that she was well, Miriam would become deeply offended that the doctor might be accusing her of malingering, and she went so far as to verbally abuse him in a most personal manner. This left her GP managing and suppressing his urge to be rude back to her. The therapist running the Balint groups that Miriam's GP attended recognised the intense transference relationship that Miriam had developed for her GP. The therapist picked up Miriam's earlier flirtatious behaviour and on the GP's feelings of isolation from his colleagues, and suggested that the engagement of a chaperone might have been experienced by Miriam as her GP's rejection of her. Therefore, it seemed possible that the verbal vituperative attack on him was a result of his intervention to resist her. Involvement of a third party seemed to have shattered the illusion of intimacy that Miriam may have harboured.

Discussion

In forensic psychiatry, there exist many examples of highly sexualised sadistic crimes which involve the control of another human with whom the perpetrator is intimately identified. The victim may get seriously injured or die from the sadistic act. In some really extreme and notable cases, even parts of their anatomy may be devoured by their attacker (Martens, 2011). This kind of sadism is associated with psychotic thinking where the internalisation of the desired object is taken literally rather than symbolically. Some theorists consider the sadistic attitude derives from a profound loneliness and an ill-directed attempt at achieving communion with another. Ruszczynski (2007) suggests that the sexualisation in a sadomasochistic encounter acts like a "binding force", securing the object relationship. Sadistic and masochistic relating militates against the experience of separateness and loneliness.

In the case illustration above, there seems to be some suggestion of excited eroticised feelings serving as a substitute for a genuine relatedness. The GP found himself the object of Miriam's intense anger and frustration at the point when he introduced the chaperone: he was not, after all, the good doctor she had previously thought he was. In her phantasy, she seemed to have created a relationship with him that was never real. During her appointments with him, the GP had picked up on her intense loneliness; perhaps this might even have resonated with his own experiences. However, the intense feelings of isolation the young GP felt in response to his colleagues' unsupportive behaviour could perhaps have been a projective identification from Miriam herself, revealing the origins of the controlling and abusive behaviour. Introducing the chaperone not only acted as a pragmatic barrier, but also broke the intense transference/countertransference relationship.

Trevor

Trevor was a man with a terminal illness who had been admitted to a hospice. Although he was physically comfortable there, he began to insist on being taken to Zurich so that he could end his life. His few friends simply could not comprehend this wish of Trevor's, and it seemed as if Trevor's sole motive was to upset these friends. He himself acknowledged that it would be more uncomfortable for him to leave the hospice and travel to Zurich, but also admitted to having hateful feelings towards his fellow men.

In this sad case, the psychotherapist who attended to Trevor established from taking his personal history during the assessment that his sadistic motives seemed derived from a long-standing sense of disconnectedness and alienation. He had felt profoundly lonely throughout his life, and in the act of pursuing assisted suicide, he had generated tremendous interest in himself: the repeated assessments from psychiatrists and psychologists had provided him with a form of intimate attention. This "wish" on his part was taken seriously by professional carers around him but, in doing so, they had experienced it as a sadistic attack on himself and on his friends rather than a pragmatic decision to reduce suffering. His rejection of his own life, and rejection of the love and friendship of his friends, could be considered as a compulsive repetition of previous trauma in which he suffered an absence of love and feelings of alienation in his childhood.

Sadistic abuse of older people in care homes

Sadistic acts of commission or omission (such as controlling or wilfully neglecting people in need) perpetrated against vulnerable older people feature in the literature of elder abuse. Garner and Evans (2000, 2002) highlighted the risks of institutional abuse committed against older people in hospitals and in nursing and residential homes. They examined the factors leading to neglect and harm caused to older adults in institutional settings. A number of aetiological risk factors were identified that can lead to less than optimum treatment of vulnerable older people, and these were pertinent to organisational factors or the institutions where the people lived, the possible difficulties brought out in the carers, and in the personalities or behaviours of the abused people themselves. Often, the dynamic between the abused and abuser was highly relevant; so, for example, if the carer believed that the older person or patient was doing something on purpose, that is, deliberately setting out to make their lives more difficult, they might become angry and retaliate at a point of crisis.

Abuse is a violation of the trust placed on carers. It is very rare for carers to set out consciously to abuse. However, it can occur in caring environments that are increasingly impoverished, such as an underfunded institution that is struggling for adequate resources and which demands much of poorly paid individuals. In these cases, the caring tasks can be rendered nigh on impossible. When care staff know their charges well, empathy and kindness more often prevail. Most care in institutions is provided with love and respect.

Institutions with a high turnover of staff and patients are much more at risk of incidents of abuse. When there is no time for carers to make attachments with those in their charge, the lives of real people can be diminished, as exemplified by phrases such as "bed-blocker" or "social admission". These terms are often used by otherwise caring clinicians or hospital managers when exasperated beyond tolerance by pressures on a flawed health and social care system.

The breakdown in care of older people has been described and high-lighted over a number of years, with various enquiries into abuse and neglect of older hospitalised patients: the Beechwood House Enquiry (1999), the North Lakes Enquiry (2004), the Mid-Staffordshire Enquiry (2013). Davenhill (2007) and Evans (2014) highlight how funding deci-sions for elderly people with dementia can get so far removed from the real people that there is a risk of a kind of loss of responsibility on behalf of commissioners forced to make choices about where the money goes and where it doesn't. There is little change from the early 1980s and 1990s, when in the United Kingdom facilities on the National Health Service (NHS) available for long-term care were closed down in favour of these being provided by the private-sector-run care homes. Government policy seemed impervious to the plight of the vulnerable residents moved from everything and everyone they had known for decades without appropriate thought or planning (Davenhill, 1998).

Using Winnicott's understanding of the development of the "capacity for concern" (1963), which builds on the Kleinian notion of the depressive position (1946), it follows that in order to be able competently and kindly to care for another, one must have the experience of being cared for. The Francis Report 2012 shone the spotlight on abusive practices in geriatric medical wards, particularly what was described as the sadistic nature of some practices. The report highlighted the need to support staff and create a nurturing environment for patients and for senior staff within the organisation to take appropriate responsibility for the provision of good care. Winnicott's 1949 paper "Hate in the counter-transference" acknowledges the ubiquitous existence of negative feelings within the relationship between the carer and the person being cared for, and it gives us permission to feel this way without using defences such as pro-jection or denial, and thus without acting harmfully.

The link with sadism is the acknowledgement that, at some level, there was satisfaction derived from the awareness that people were suffering. In this case, it is hugely unlikely that satisfaction would be experienced consciously; the exertion of power, however inappropriate, may counter feelings of low self-esteem in the perpetrator. The major-ity of nursing and health-care support staff would deny ever feeling so negatively about their patients, and certainly would do nothing to jeopardise their relationship of caring, however, given sufficient provocation, who amongst us so-called normal people are completely innocent of negative feelings towards others?

Sadism in the loneliness of ageing and sickness

Sadism is not just a behaviour of disturbed people, it is a part of the normal human experience which needs the civilising influence of parental nurture and ultimately societal sanction and support to prevent its expression in a way that is damaging to others.

Feeling disgust and dismay is normal; for example, it is understandable that we feel disgust at cleaning up vomit or faeces. However, disgust and dismay are also experienced in relation to the ageing process itself, and to a greater extent towards frailty and dementia. Our Western culture that appears to value and worship youth over age has (at some point) to contend with the reality of the human condition: that we age, we get sick, and we die.

Klein described a "state of internal loneliness" (1963, pp. 300–313) in which she moots a yearning for a perfect internal state, which is unachievable. Klein linked this state with the depressive and schizoid anxieties of infancy but which return with greater force in adult life during periods of illness.

In his elegant paper on the loneliness in old age, Noel Hess (1987) uses Shakespeare's King Lear to illustrate how the narcissistic wounding of ageing is offset unconsciously by the elderly king who divides his kingdom amongst his family—acknowledging that he is old and giving up his throne while still demanding absolute loyalty from them, that is, still exercising control. The two elder daughters, while feigning allegiance, behave increasingly cruelly and sadistically towards him, which leaves him ultimately destitute and evidently vulnerable.

Sadistic behaviour towards frail older people who are vulnerable is also explained by psychoanalytic understanding as an attack on the frail, disgusting, and unloved parts of ourselves, un-owned and denied by us, projected into our vulnerable charges in a horrible, mindless, and thoughtless evacuation of uncomfortable feelings. The psychoanalytic stance on this range of feelings is that they are largely unconscious and represent the darker, shadowy side of the human psyche. Ways of making them conscious through psychotherapy include getting people to talk about a situation that is causing them anxiety, or about a patient or person about whom we feel stuck. Senior people in the caring professions can model good practice by acknowledging that they feel less than positive about a person or a situation but taking care to maintain high professional standards at all times.

Understanding our own sadistic feelings, acknowledging them as part of all of us, and taking steps to reduce the risk of their emergence, is a governance issue for all care institutions, including the NHS. If we do so, we are far less likely to retaliate or to behave sadistically or unprofessionally towards patients.

Psychological abuse of the elderly

This is far more common than direct physical or sexual abuse of vulnerable older people.

It can seem relatively innocuous and occurs frequently in the domestic caring setting. It is an abuse of power that tends to happen in a complicated dynamic between people who have known each other for a while. Threatening to put a frail relative in an old peoples' home might occur occasionally when an exhausted carer is at the end of their tether. This is understandable, even though it is not considered as good practice. However, it is far less likely to occur if that carer is supported properly, both practically and emotionally. Repeatedly threatening the elderly whilst enjoying the power is sadistic, as is ignoring pleas for help when an individual needs assistance.

Pillemer and Moore (1989) surveyed five hundred and fifty-seven nurses in American institutions who were able to disclose witnessing or perpetrating physical abuse and psychological abuse of their aged charges. These feelings are not restricted to the few. They are experienced by many carers who admit to these feelings when seeking help and support, although, of course, they may not act. It is formal and informal support that will often prevent harm occurring.

Dave

Dave, a charming man in his fifties with an advanced young-onset fronto-temporal dementia, looked his new doctor in the eye when, at the end of a consultation, the GP offered him his hand. Dave squeezed the doctor's hand to a degree beyond tolerance. The GP yelled out in pain, extricating himself forcefully from the grip. All the while his patient was grinning and continued in a friendly way but seemed to be aware that he had caused pain. Where had that come from? The doctor was there to help and had not consciously provoked his patient. The frontal-lobe deterioration removed Dave's normal social control and judgement of a situation. The impulse to hurt is perhaps understandable; a relatively young man with dementia might feel rivalrous and envious of another who is well. He may have wished to exert control or dominance when he could, because he felt able to do so. Frontal and temporal dementia can provide that *carte blanche* mentality so that a behaviour is enacted which would never be entertained in health.

Discussion

It could be considered also that perhaps the young GP did provoke Dave. Besides being young and clever, perhaps he was also slightly patronising or dismissive. Maybe he chose instead to address Dave's attractive wife instead of speaking directly to his patient. This additional information might help us to understand the sadistic act. There may also have been an element of identification and an enhanced intimacy between the two men as a result of this rivalry. It may also be conjectured that Dave communicated something through a projective identification. His sense of hurt and humiliation has certainly been passed on to his clinician. The question here too might be whether there was some sadistic intent from the doctor, although.it is most likely that he didn't consciously mean any harm to Dave.

Addressing the question of loneliness might also be pertinent here. Dementia had irrevocably changed Dave's relationship with his wife, and their capacity for intimacy had been disturbed beyond recognition. Finding reasons for a new sadism is not hard; and the frontal-lobe impairment will have facilitated the enactment normally out of character for this person. Discussing the case with his supervisor might, however, have helped the doctor to understand a psychological dynamic to which he would probably be more sensitive in future.

Summary

The existence of sadistic feelings extends to older people of course. They may display sadistic tendencies in relationships as a result of a trait in their personality structure; this, as object-relations theorists have suggested, is likely to have a particular origin in early infancy and the interaction with the primary caregiver. All relationships are tinged with some ambivalence, and the extent to which a person is disturbed by sadistic feelings is likely to be a delicate balance between their desires and needs being met and their ability to manage frustration when these are not. We know that people may behave more sadistically as a result of ageing and illness in a defence against the narcissistic rage of physical insults on a fragile ego. It may also be a defence against an overwhelming sense of loneliness.

Sadism is not a particularly helpful interaction style and is likely to impact negatively on the person expressing these feelings and behaving sadistically. Older people when ill or suffering from dementia are also more vulnerable to sadistic attacks from others, particularly from those in a conflicted caring role. What is evident and important is the acknowledgement of the existence of some sadism in many human interactions and the awareness of particular situations where it is likely to cause real harm.

References

Balint, M. (1957). *The Doctor, His Patient and the Illness*. London: Pitman Medical Publishing.

Beech House Inquiry Report (1999). Camden and Islington Community Mental Health Services, London.

Davenhill, R. (1998). No truce with the Furies. *Journal of Social Work Practice, 12*: 149–157.

Davenhill, R. (2007). No truce with the Furies: issues of containment in the provision of care for people with dementia and those who care for them. In: R. Davenhill (Ed.), *Looking into Later Life: A Psychoanalytic Approach to Depression and Dementia in Old Age* (pp. 62–74). London: Karnac.

Evans, S. (2014). What the National Dementia Strategy forgot: providing dementia care from a psychodynamic perspective. *Psychoanalytic Psychotherapy, 28*: 321–329.

Francis, R. (2010). *The Mid-Staffordshire National Health Service Foundation Trust Public Enquiry Report to the House of Commons*. Department of Health.

Francis, R. (2013). *The Mid-Staffordshire National Health Service Foundation Trust Public Enquiry: Government Response*. Department of Health.

Freud, S. (1905d). *Three Essays on the Theory of Sexuality. S. E., 7*. London: Hogarth.

Freud, S. (1920g). *Beyond the Pleasure Principle. S. E., 18.* London: Hogarth.

Garner, J., & Evans, S. (2000). The institutional abuse of older adults. Council Report CR84, June. Royal College of Psychiatrists, London.

Garner, J., & Evans, S. (2002). An ethical perspective on institutional abuse of older adults. *Psychiatric Bulletin, 26:* 164–166.

Hess, N. (1987). King Lear and some anxieties of old age. *British Journal of Medical Psychology, 60:* 2019–2216.

Hess, N. (2004). Loneliness in old age: Klein and others. In: S. Evans & J. Garner (Eds.), *Talking over the Years: A Handbook of Dynamic Psychotherapy with Older Adults* (pp. 19–27). Hove, East Sussex: Brunner-Routledge.

Klein, M. (1946). Notes on some schizoid mechanisms. *International Journal of Psycho-Analysis, 27:* 99–110.

Klein, M. (1963). On the sense of loneliness. In: *Envy and Gratitude, and Other Works: 1946–1963* (pp. 300–313). London: Virago Press, 1983.

Krafft-Ebing, R. (1898). *Psychopathia Sexualis.* Stuttgart: Enke.

Laplanche, J., & Pontalis, J.-B. (1973). *The Language of Psycho-Analysis.* London: Hogarth.

Martens, W. J. (2011). Sadism linked to loneliness: psychodynamic dimensions of the sadistic serial killer Jeffrey Dahmer. *Psychoanalytic Review, 98:* 493–514.

Pillemer, K., & Moore, D. W. (1989). Abuse of patients in nursing homes: findings from a survey of staff. *Gerontology, 29:* 314–320.

Ruszczynski, S. (2007). The problem of certain psychic realities. In: D. H. Morgan & S. Ruszczynski (Eds.), *Lectures on Violence, Perversion and Delinquency: The Portman Papers* (pp. 23–42). London: Karnac.

Winnicott, D. W. (1949). Hate in the countertransference. *Internationl Journal of Psycho-Analysis, 30:* 69–74.

Winnicott, D. W. (1963). The development of the capacity for concern. *Bulletin of the Menninger Clinic, 27:* 167–176.

INDEX

9781782206378